D1237622

RACIAL TRAITS
OF
AMERICAN BLACKS

ABOUT THE AUTHOR

Kenneth M. Binkley lives in Oxford, Mississippi with his wife Deborah K. King. He has B.S., M.S., and Ph.D. degrees from Indiana State, Florida State, and the University of Tennessee, respectively. He periodically presents papers to the American Association of Physical Anthropologists and is a member of the Human Biology Council. Previously active in southeastern archaeology, he has completed several major projects for the University of Mississippi. An aviator and former analyst in aviation systems, he has been principal investigator in research projects for NASA and the armed forces. He has traveled extensively in Europe, North Africa, and the Caribbean. A lieutenant-commander in the navy, he was honorably discharged in 1970. Now 52 and semi-retired, Mr. Binkley spends most of his time writing and engaged in his own research projects.

RACIAL TRAITS
OF
AMERICAN BLACKS

By

KENNETH M. BINKLEY, PH.D.

CHARLES C THOMAS • PUBLISHER
Springfield • Illinois • U.S.A.

Published and Distributed Throughout the World by

CHARLES C THOMAS • PUBLISHER
2600 South First Street
Springfield, Illinois 62794-9265

© *1989 by* CHARLES C THOMAS • PUBLISHER
ISBN 0-398-55599-8
Library of Congress Catalog Card Number: 89-4600

With THOMAS BOOKS *careful attention is given to all details of manufacturing
and design. It is the Publisher's desire to present books that are satisfactory as to their
physical qualities and artistic possibilities and appropriate for their particular use.*
THOMAS BOOKS *will be true to those laws of quality that assure a good name
and good will.*

Printed in the United States of America
SC-R-3

Library of Congress Cataloging-in-Publication Data

Binkley, Kenneth M.
     Racial traits of American Blacks / by Kenneth M. Binkley.
          p.   cm.
     Bibliography: p.
     ISBN 0-398-05599-8
     1. Afro-Americans—Anthropology. 2. Black race. I. Title.
GN57.A35B56   1989
572' .896073—dc20   89-4600
                                                                                     CIP

PREFACE

After completing this book the reader should appreciate the importance of race and should have a solid concept of why races exist. He or she will also be able to distinguish myth from reality with respect to many specific racial features of American Blacks. These features are not exhausted herein, but certainly the more important ones, and the ones which generate the most questions, are addressed. The presentation here also should consign any feeling of racial pride or prejudice to its appropriate status of being just plain silly.

The book is about the racial features of Black Americans. Primarily it addresses the same old questions about the traits of Blacks, questions which seem to persist in spite of the last twenty or so years of racial integration. Are Whites more intelligent than Blacks? Are Blacks better athletes? Are Blacks' heads harder, making them more difficult to knock to the canvas? Do Blacks have more muscles? Do Black people sink and White people float? What about the fabled penis size of the Black male? Are Blacks naturally better dancers than Whites? By no means are these rare questions asked by an uninformed few; rather, they seem to reflect the present understanding of Black racial characteristics. They are all addressed herein and should satisfy the reader's curiosity about most traits of Black Americans, if not all of them. But the book is more than a parade of racial traits which have been established by authorities on the subject. In an attempt to show why racial prejudice is illogical, I provide some discussion on the origin of race and the functions of racial traits. I also delve into racial information to arrive at conclusions which fairly well isolate me on the proverbial limb. These proposed traits are properly labeled as controversial. Most of them have to do with early development. The reader is free to try to saw off the limb or to join me as she or he pleases.

I believe that the biological aspect of race needs to be emphasized anew, and I hope this book will have some effect in that direction. The recent attempt to sweep away the social implications of racial features seems to be also undermining what already has been learned about the biology of race. Today, the social ideal is to neglect racial features, to consider them as unimportant biological stamps. Already a knee jerk reaction seems to ensue when some disease or disorder is discovered to be more frequent in a particular race: the initial response is to seek an explanation solely in terms of socioeconomics. A similar reaction occurs when medical treatment is discovered to be unequal among the races: it is automatically attributed to racial prejudice without any investigation whatsoever into the biology of the matter. Further, there seems to be a popular notion that once America's wealth is equitably distributed among her citizens, then biological factors such as mortality rates, diseases, birthweights, frequencies of malformation, growth rates, and overall health and life span will also fall into line. This is a disturbing trend, and I believe that the pendulum has swung too far in the opposite direction. It is desirable to disregard race from a social perspective. But to ignore all its aspects is to neglect genetic processes which have been operating since the dawn of modern human beings. The fact is, there are biological differences among the races. These have direct influence on factors such as disease type and incidence, life span, birth defect frequency, tooth decay, and a host of others. These differences want continuing investigation on a fine scale. The findings need to be widely disseminated. Presently, there is some danger that they will be swept under the rug for the sake of social decorum.

Hopefully, this exposition of Black racial features will encourage some readers to pursue studies involving the biology of race. But if it serves no more purpose than to encourage a lively and more learned discussion about race, unencumbered by a load of pride and prejudice, then my efforts will have been amply rewarded.

K. M. BINKLEY

CONTENTS

RACIAL TRAITS
OF
AMERICAN BLACKS

1

INTRODUCTION

I don't know why we anthropologists are so reluctant to publicize what we have learned. It's not like we would be into hear-and-tell for big bucks, the route many national leaders and their servants and housemaids have made trendy in recent years. Indeed, years of anthropological research often has little value outside of public dissemination. We often hear "The Indians used to . . . ," and successfully suppress a snicker at what follows. The tearful television Indian brave who gazes balefully at the beer cans and fast-food wraps bobbing along the backwaters probably has at least half the viewers believing that native Americans were one big family of conservationists. Meanwhile, we anthropologists sneak a gloating peep at each other, knowing that at least two hundred tribes were romping around when Columbus made his appearance, most of them imbued with intense hatred for each other, slaughtering mammals for hides and birds for plummage, polluting to the limits their primitive technologies would allow, speaking some fifty-odd different languages, some as mutually unintelligible as modern French and ancient Hebrew.

We have publicized some knowledge. For example, early in American history, there was a notion that the New World had been inhabited by a race of giants. That idea was so thoroughly debunked by the first anthropologists that not many people even know of it today. Largely because of the teaching of anthropologists, the idea of hanging white shirts and woolen suits on natives of the rain forest now seems ridiculous. The notion that Friday would rush headlong to embrace the English culture of Robinson Crusoe—in his own native land, to boot—now borders on the absurd. Customs and social practices different from our own are no longer considered trivial or scornful or humorous. In fact, the global expanse of business enterprise today demands that foreign representatives learn and avoid behavior which might be offensive to people of other cultures.

But concepts of race are still archaic, and anthropologists have failed

3

to speak out on the subject. One of the most prevalent fancies, probably bolstered by the social movements of the 1960s, is that race is some sort of biological veneer; beneath, human beings are all the same. Others see races as various degradations in the ideal human form which was created at the start of humankind. In Europe, particularly France, the word "savage" still conjures up visions of natural nobility, strength, and keen senses. Races often are conceived as "breeds" of people, as easily sortable as hounds and terriers.

Anthropologists are not totally to blame for this sorry state of understanding of what race is all about. It has been extremely unpopular to air what knowledge we do have. To allude to the possibility that race might influence performance in this or that endeavor can, and has, cost jobs. At least in America, to identify the race of an individual in print has become tantamount to contempt, no matter whether he or she is a child molester or a champion in the Olympic Games. Certainly, no course of study on race is required for a baccalaureate degree in any American educational institution, nor is one likely to be required in the near future. Further, most of us are ignorant of most of our own racial features.

I think this overly sensitive attitude toward race is changing, especially with respect to Black Americans. Blacks increasingly are becoming part of the "we" and less of the "they." Black military officers of high rank are no longer rare. Widespread Black participation in traditionally White sports now has considerable time depth. Joe Louis, Jesse Owens, and Jackie Robinson are dead. Milt Campbell, Bill Russell, and Wilt Chamberlain are middle-aged and retired. Some current Black athletes are carrying on the professions of their fathers, and in a few cases, their fathers and grandfathers. Bill Cosby is eagerly awaited in all homes, as the ratings prove, and White boys have begged for "Mr. T" haircuts. Anybody would have to be blind or very dull not to perceive the Black influence on dance, music, and certain sports. The lingering question which bothers Whites is whether or not the success of Blacks in these fields is grounded in their racial heritage. The time seems right to publicize what anthropologists know about the racial features of Black Americans.

Facing the television on a leisurely Sunday afternoon, watching basketball or football with neighbors and other acquaintances, I hear the most remarkable beliefs about the Black players. One time, an incredible runback merely generated the mundane remark that any Black, being out of the jungle only a few generations, could be expected to execute such an unusually skillful performance. Not long ago, I was informed—all anatomy texts to the contrary—that Blacks have an "extra muscle" in each leg which helps them run faster than Whites. The important point is that ideas such as these come from the lips of attorneys, architects, engineers and other educated professionals who claim no particular racial prejudice. Not surprisingly, most of this nonsense is prefaced apathetically by "I have heard that..." or "Blacks are supposed to have...," as if accurate information is so obscure that it is useless to attempt a refutation or verification. Columnist Lewis Grizzard has offered up "White Man's Disease" as a humorous explanation for the alleged superiority of Blacks in basketball. To appreciate the humor is also to suspect a grain of truth. Recently, I noticed in the Sunday comics one character ruminating on the possibility that race makes Blacks better dancers than Whites. Clearly, there seems to be an increasing interest in just who Blacks really are.

I have written this little book in an attempt to provide, in one or two sittings, much of what is known about the racial features of American Blacks. Nothing herein is new, but I have looked at some old and some new information from a different perspective. In that way I hope to have functioned as something more than a parrot. I have also tried to offer more than a mere list of known racial features. The origin, maintenance, and ramifications of racial traits are complex, and I have tried in the chapter following this introduction to give the reader some appreciation of what these are all about. The third chapter concerns probably the most important and certainly the most controversial racial traits, yet they are not generally recognized as racial features at all. These are the racial peculiarities of Blacks in early development. They include factors such as birthweights, the way toxins affect birthweights, birth defects, tooth development, and the development of fingerprints. I have stated my view on what these features mean and then support this view with specific information from relevant sources. Data sources for birthweights and the effect of tobacco toxins in Blacks and Whites come from the work of S. M. Garn, who used the same information for different purposes. The raw data for birth defects are from works by J. D. Erickson, G. M. Heathcote, J. D. Niswander and associates, A. P. Polednak, and M. B. Roche with G. G. Rowe. The birth defect data provided by S. Taffel is credited and explained in A. P. Polednak's work which is identified in the bibliography at the end of this book. S. M. Garn, R. Jordan, B. S. Kraus, and D. F. Roberts are among the investigators who conducted the landmark studies on racial differences in tooth development. I have more or less just reported the parts of their work which support my views on racial differences in early development of the human body. W. J. Babler kindly provided me with unpublished data from his work on finger ridge analysis, data which add a great deal of strength to my conclusions on the early development of Blacks. The fourth chapter is about the racial features of Black youth and adults. These traits are banal to social scientists but tend to be of paramount interest to others because they are mostly visible features. Skull topography, body density, body proportions, limb lengths and intrinsic proportions, pelvic breadth, and soft tissue features such as hair type, penis size, and lip morphology are included. I have used books by W. M. Bass and W. M. Krogman to cover the skeletal features, and the work of A. M. Brues to discuss several soft tissue features. Technical articles by R. M. Malina have provided growth data, and a recent publication by S. R. Vickery has been useful in verifying body density. Interviews with prostitutes provided information on penis size. All of these sources have been indispensable in the preparation of Chapter 4 on the features of youth and adulthood. The succeeding chapter, on intelligence and athletics, employs information on basketball scores which was provided by the Sports Information Offices of the Universities of Alabama, Georgia, and Mississippi. The discussion in Chapter 5 is fairly well my own, and it relies heavily on reasonable assumptions, based on knowledge and experience, for the conclusions reached. The sixth chapter is a short exposition on how some of the racial features of Blacks may have originated. The whole concept of this chapter belongs to R. L. Jantz. Although he has briefly mentioned the idea in his published work, Jantz has used the concept mainly as a dialectic in the anthropology classroom where I at one time sat. The final chapter contains specific information on American Black and White admixture, and this data is based on the studies of B. S. Blumberg, P. L. Workman, and their associates. Any mistakes in interpreting the information used in any of the chapters are my own.

I trust that my use of the term "Black" will be acceptable to the reader. No single word seems to satisfy everybody for very long. I have always thought that "Negro" could be bastardized too easily. "Afro-American" is not very definitive, because Africa is occupied by more than one race. "Colored" is suffused with too much social inflammation. But "Black" snaps out crisply and cleanly no matter whose mouth pronounces it, the word cannot be bastardized and still make any sense, and it is reminiscent of the late 1960s and early 1970s, when it felt good just to be an American.

The language here is non-technical. Many figures are included, and the reader can get much of the book's message by merely reading the captions and examining the figures. I believe that the book offers an adequate and painless introduction to the racial features of Black Americans. The only purpose of the book is to raise the level of consciousness of what being Black is, in a biological sense. The thrust of the message is fourfold: one, all people are more alike than different, regardless of race; two, the differences which do exist among races are not superficial; three, there are natural causes for racial differences; and four, these causes are discoverable.

2

WHAT RACE MEANS

Explanation of race is the province of the physical anthropologist. To briefly summarize his or her universe of interest, I think most anthropologists would agree, based on geography, on five for the number of the world's major races. These are the American Indians native to North and South America; the Caucasians, distributed in a roughly circular area around the Mediterranean Sea, including North Africa and West Asia; the Mongoloids of East Asia, including Mongolia, China, Japan, and parts of Siberia; the Negroes, native to Africa south of the Sahara Desert; and the Oceanians, distributed on the islands in the South Pacific. Every race is composed of a number of human groups, each of which is somewhat different from all others, so certainly not every anthropologist would agree on the total number of races or where to draw the line between the major races. Some would even define hundreds of races, based on minute physical differences, and be completely justified in doing so. But for the purposes of this book, it is sufficient to go with the lowest number possible and point out the degree of overlap among the major races of interest here.

The anthropologist perceives race as sort of an up-to-date summary of past events, not as a basic difference between types of people. There are no completely separable types of people, only human features which appear more or less frequently from one group of people to another. In the past, the five major groups of humans have been fairly well isolated from each other by geography. This insularity has caused biological features which occur in every human group to occur more frequently in one of the major groups than in the other four, or vice versa. Different climates and resources, different social laws for producing offspring, variability in migration and immigration, and different levels of technology protecting people from their unique environments all add up over the generations, eventually producing higher or lower frequencies of particular physical features. More often than not, the physical features which become more common in a people are the ones most suited to the climate of their geographic area. This has led anthropologists to theorize that humans who have physical characters which are well-suited to a particular region generate more offspring than people who don't. Thus, the genes which are responsible for producing these desirable features become more common in the group which can use them. It comes as no surprise that certain racial characters often make good sense with respect to the prevailing climate in the inhabited region. Still, when the anthropologist measures a feature such as nose size or skin color or the frequency of a certain blood type, only the average is larger or smaller in one race than in others. Features of the same size, the same blood types, and identical skin color can be found in all other races to some extent. Only the prevalence varies. So, there are no absolute biological boundaries between any two races.

In spite of the high degree of overlap in physical features among the races, the natural tendency is to think of race in terms of stereotypes, frequently inaccurate ones. Short stature and flat faces are features of Mongoloids, while tallness and a sharp face are two traits characteristic of Caucasians. Thus, the stereotypical Chinese person in our society is short, round, and featureless. Similarly, the stereotypical Caucasian by Chinese standards is a gawky giant whose face sticks out like an axe blade. In the flesh, individuals often fail to cooperate by not falling into line with the stereotype. For those who missed the Chinese exhibit at the 1982 World's Fair, it was in charge of a lean Chinese man roughly seven feet tall. Probably most Chinese don't recognize that American baseball great Babe Ruth had a nose shape which is common among Negroes and a face as flat as many Mongoloids. Say the word "Eskimo" and most Americans see a short, fat, flat-nosed little fellow. In fact, Eskimos have long, narrow noses and more muscle per unit of fat than most American citizens. It is desirable to overcome the tendency to perceive people in terms of stereotypes and to recognize that biological features of individuals always crosscut the races to some extent. Given an individual body and nothing else to go on, the race of the individual often cannot be identified. Humans just cannot be sorted so simply into "breeds" like dogs. This truism is emphasized throughout this book.

Since we Americans now carry out most of our lives indoors, climate is often underrated as an agent of biological change. Yet even in our society Minnesotans occasionally freeze to death while Floridians never do. If the people residing in these states could be isolated from each other for an indefinitely long period of time, some biological differences between them would become evident. Presumably, in the distant past, technology provided less protection from the elements than it does today. Biological adaptation must have been more important and must have proceeded at a faster rate.

Climate not only exerts direct effects on human beings. It, along with the geology of a region, also dictates what plants and animals will and will not flourish. Thus, climate affects the resources available for human consumption, the nourishment they provide, and the biological price that they exact for consuming them. For example, many generations of West Africans have been eating foods containing low levels of deadly cyanide. Physical anthropologists are just now beginning to study the impact of this historical dosage on the present genetic structure of West Africans. Another example which has recently come to light is the ethnic distribution of diabetes. Many American Indians lived an active life, of normal span for the times, never knowing that they had diet-controllable diabetes. After Europeans arrived and changed the food resources from high protein to high sugar and carbohydrate, diabetes became, and is, widespread in the American Indian population. It is easy to see how, over thousands of years, some genetic response to the climate of a geographic area would occur, and certain physical features would accumulate in the natives.

It should be emphasized again that races are not types of people. In the not-too-distant past, anthropologists probably were guilty of grandstanding in regard to racial features, and unwittingly promoted the idea of types of people. Consider a statement to the effect that native Australians have teeth so large and strong that they can sharpen their stone tools with them. This is the sort of reporting that captures the imagination and conjures up images of a people so different from you and I that every one of them can chew rocks. Unfortunately, few readers insist on answers to the more specific questions such as exactly how many people were observed thus sharpening their tools, what were the conditions which required such behavior, how many cracked teeth were the result, how many natives regarded the procedure as sheer idiocy, and what is the frequency of individuals in other races who also can sharpen stone tools with the teeth? The fact is, for every race known on earth, the people within it are biologically more different from each other than the average of one race is different from the average of another race. To illustrate, skin color can be used as an example. In this book, the terms "Black" and "White" are used in place of the more cumbersome "Negro" and "Caucasian." Here in America, most Blacks are more black than white, and most Whites are more white than black, thus the name for each group is appropriate. But this nomenclature sometimes promotes the misconception that all Caucasians are white and all Negroes are black. Nothing could be farther from the truth. The existence of American Blacks and Whites is an accidental outcome of historical events. Negroid skin color varies from nearly white in East Africa to nearly black in West Africa. Because of the prevailing slave trade routes, all but about 2 percent of American Blacks originated in West Africa where the skin is unusually dark. Caucasoid skin color varies between very dark brown in West Asia to nearly white in West Europe. By chance, most American Whites came from West Europe where the skin is unusually light. The average difference in skin color between the two races is not nearly as great as the differences within each race, or the difference between American Blacks and Whites. If America had been settled by West Asian Caucasians, who in turn had imported Negro slaves from East Africa, the terms "Black" and "White" could not be used except arbitrarily.

At this point, mention of racial pride might be in order. Science fiction writers have the habit of populating their spaceships with beings from different planets. The home planet of a crew member dictates his or her capabilities and limitations. For example, Mr. Spock is gifted with superior logic but feels no emotions. The Wookiee has superior size and strength but cannot speak. Superman is superstrong except in the presence of kryptonite. The sci-fi audience seems to accept these fanciful biological features as the normal state of affairs. But any mention that a real person might be better or worse at this or that because of his or her racial roots is considered to be a statement of outright heresy. The truth is, ethnic and racial origin does affect the probability that certain superiorities and inferiorities will occur in an individual. If you are an Eskimo, the chances are good that you can bite me harder than I can bite you. On average, Eskimos have the strongest jaws in the world. If you are Irish, the probability is high that I can withstand more direct sunlight on my bare skin than you can on yours. If you are native to Australia, you probably use less cover on a cool night than I do. Unfortunately, or perhaps fortunately, in spite of these racial superiorities in very specific instances, everything evens out in the end. No race enjoys any overall superiority over another. Biology works on the genes in such a way that there is always a payback. Animal breeders are keenly aware of how a solution also tends to cause another problem. Dogs bred for a specific purpose, for example, also have notable weaknesses. Doberman pinschers have excellent watchdog features, but they are limited by weak hips and short life spans. In humans, comparable processes are at work. Any racial feature has potential negative impact in several ways. For one, adaptive features which work well at one time often go haywire at a later time. Fast healing of flesh wounds is desirable in the jungle where microorganisms flourish. Rapid repair of torn flesh is characteristic of young Blacks who are products of a jungle existence. The same process apparently increases the frequency of lupus, scleroderma, and other connective tissue disorders in Blacks of middle age. Also, racial characters desirable in one climate often don't work very well in another. Irish skins absorb a lot of the precious few sunrays in their owners' homeland. But the Irish are prone to skin cancer if they happen to migrate to America. Probably the biggest payback is that most diseases, especially constitutional diseases, have a more or less unique ethnic distribution such that they occur more frequently in some races and ethnic groups than in others. For example, Tay-Sachs syndrome occurs most frequently in Jews, but tuberculosis among Jews is fairly infrequent. Generally, the incidences of constitutional diseases such as rheumatoid arthritis, psoriasis, muscular dystrophy, diabetes, and so forth, cannot be explained by diet and environment. The present thinking is that such inborn maladies must have a lot to do with genetic heritage. This heritage in turn has everything to do with race. So if you feel that your race has conferred some sort of special advantage on you, don't count on feeling that way too long.

3

BLACK RACIAL FEATURES
AND THE EARLY STAGES OF LIFE

Introduction. Birthweight is not usually thought of as a racial feature. There is no doubt, however, that Blacks are born smaller than babies of other races, whether they are born in America or Europe or Africa. Exactly why this is true is in dispute. Many investigators attribute the condition to low socioeconomic status. The hypothesis proposed here is that Blacks are born smaller because they undergo a slower, more accurate period of development.

Evidence increasingly points to a slow developmental period in Blacks. If this proves to be true, a lower birthweight would be the logical outcome. Some of this research is old, and none of it was conducted for the specific purpose of demonstrating slower development in Blacks. Nevertheless, when presented in cumulative form, the results are impressive. Older research on tooth development and growth indicates a slower developmental period in Blacks, and newer research on fingerprints strongly supports this indication. Further, data on birth defects seem to demonstrate that large birthweights among Blacks represent an abnormal and undesirable condition. Each line of evidence is presented below.

Birthweight, Race, and Maternal Weight. The birthweight of a baby is highly correlated with the normal, prepregnancy weight of the mother. As the average weight increases in a group of women, so does the likelihood that they will produce babies of larger average birthweights. Figure 1 demonstrates the positive correlation between birthweight and maternal weight in American Blacks and Whites. As shown in the figure, a group of mothers who all weigh eighty-five pounds will produce babies whose birthweights average either 3120 grams or 2860 grams, depending upon whether the group is Black or White. This is not to say that each White baby weighs 3120 grams and each Black baby weighs 2860 grams at birth. In fact, the birthweights overlap between the races and among the mothers. The reader is no doubt thinking of a small mother who gave

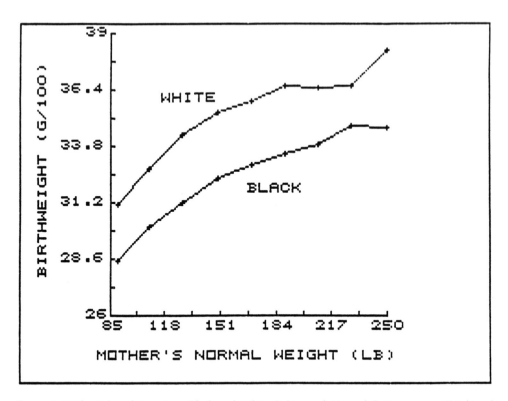

Figure 1. Birthweights of American Black and White Babies and Normal Prepregnancy Weights of Their Mothers.

In most cases, a baby's weight at birth can be predicted by the normal weight of the mother. In large samples, a group of mothers whose weight is low will produce a group of small babies. In this figure, the birthweights of a large sample of American babies are plotted against their mothers' normal weights.

For any given prepregnancy weight of both Black and White mothers, the American Black baby is born smaller than the White baby. However, this phenomenon is not confined to Americans. Blacks appear to have the world's smallest birthweights, regardless of their present domicile.

birth to a huge baby. This is expected. But in large samples, the average birthweight figures hold up and point to a real racial difference in birthweights.

A low birthweight is, in itself, of little consequence. But a racial disposition toward lower birthweights has important ramifications. For one thing, birthweight is almost always invoked as a measure of the well-being of newborns. The terms "big" and "healthy" are synonymous in the minds of lay persons and medical practitioners alike. For another, among anthropologists, there is academic interest in any racial characteristic, because it usually signals some important geographic or climatic condition which prevailed in the past. Finally, to define "abnormal" and "normal," it may be necessary to devise separate birthweight standards for Blacks and Whites.

Studies of Tooth Development. Several studies of tooth development suggest that Blacks develop more slowly than other races. One study conducted around twenty years ago involved the measurement of tooth buds. These are the very first mineral deposits which eventually grow into deciduous or "baby" teeth. The subjects, unborn American Indian and Black babies, ranged in age from twelve to twenty-five weeks after conception.

Figure 2 shows the size of the first deciduous molar bud in successively older Black and American Indian babies. The diverging lines indicate that as age increases, the molar tooth bud grows proportionately larger in American Indian babies. Although additional tooth buds were observed in the study, the growth rates were virtually identical to the first molar shown here.

The big question is, of course, whether or not tooth buds represent the rest of the body in the rate of growth and development. It is known that adult American Indians have larger teeth than adult Blacks. Critics could argue that tooth development rate is unique, and the normally larger teeth in American Indians are evident right from the start. This is a valid criticism, but it is rather weak in the light of other evidence. At birth, the weight of the Black baby is smaller than the American Indian, and the developing teeth have smaller dimensions. The stronger argument is that the Black baby has developed more slowly.

Another study of deciduous tooth development involved living Black and White children. The investigators counted the number of teeth erupted through the gums in groups of American Black and White children aged six months, nine months, twelve months, and nineteen months. For each age group, Whites averaged more teeth than Blacks. By nine months Whites scored between three and four teeth to the Black group's two to three. At twelve months, Whites averaged six teeth and Blacks between four and five. By nineteen months Whites had twelve to thirteen teeth compared to a Black score of eleven. Figure 3 graphically portrays the outcome of the tooth eruption research.

It is too bad that American Indians, Blacks, and Whites all were not observed in both of the studies. As it stands, the first study doesn't say if both White and American Indian unborns are ahead of Black unborns in

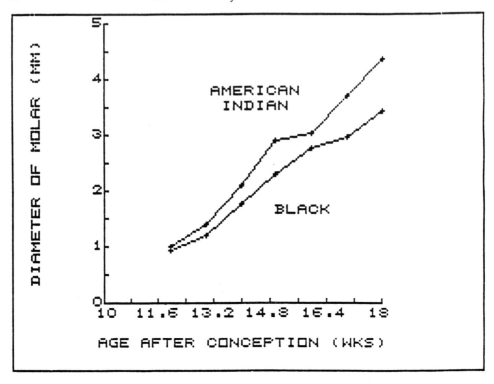

Figure 2. Diameter of Molar Tooth Buds in Unborn Black and American Indian Babies of Different Ages.

The dimension of the first deciduous (baby) molar is shown for several ages. The deciduous teeth begin to form in the jaw bones long before the baby is born. When the molar first becomes measurable, it is already slightly larger in American Indians than in Blacks. Notice that as the age after conception increases, the tooth bud becomes progressively larger in American Indians. This faster growth rate in American Indians is shown by the diverging lines. A slower growth rate in the baby teeth may be one indication that Blacks develop more slowly overall in the early stages than babies of other races.

tooth bud development, and the second study doesn't say if both American Indian and White children are ahead of Black children in tooth eruption. However, there is some indirect evidence that tends to alleviate the problem. As demonstrated in Figure 3, at some time between nineteen months and two years of age, a definite crossover in tooth eruption rate occurs between Black and White children. From that age onward, Blacks erupt the remaining deciduous teeth and all the permanent teeth on an earlier schedule than do Whites. Figure 4 shows the eruption schedule for the permanent teeth in American Blacks and Whites.

It is clear that a distinct growth rate crossover of Black versus White children occurs at about two years of age. Thus, it is unlikely that unborn Blacks would be ahead of White unborns in tooth bud development.

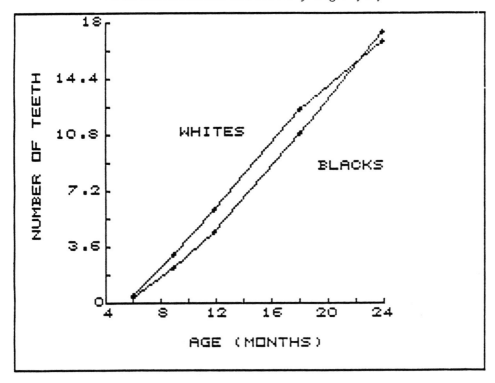

Figure 3. Number of Deciduous Teeth Which Have Erupted Through the Gums of Black and White Children from Six Months to Two Years of Age.

On the average, Black children have fewer teeth showing in the mouth until the age of about nineteen months. Between nineteen months and two years, a developmental crossover occurs, and Blacks begin to exhibit more deciduous teeth than Whites. The lagging number of teeth erupted in Blacks provides another source of evidence that there is a racial difference in the rates of overall development in the early stages. A slight upturn can be distinguished in the Black line between twelve months and two years, and a slight downturn in the White line after sixteen months.

Repeated crossovers, where first one race leads, then the other, then the first again, and so forth, are virtually unknown. Either zero or one crossover is the general rule for any one structure or tissue. Therefore, it is highly probable that the crossover shown in Figure 3 is the only one which occurs between Blacks and Whites. It seems likely that Blacks lag behind Whites and American Indians, both in the early phases of tooth bud development and in tooth eruption, up to about two years of age.

It is important to recognize that a considerable degree of overlap exists between the races in tooth development and eruption. A significant amount of individual variation is always evident in biological processes, regardless of what feature is being measured. Teeth are no exception. One would not expect to find more deciduous teeth in every individual White one-year-old than in every Black of the same age. Nor would one find that all Blacks get their permanent molars before all Whites. In fact, the two individuals with the most and least developed teeth could be either Black or White, just as the tallest person in the world doesn't necessarily have to originate in a family, ethnic group, or race whose members are typically tall. It is the difference between group averages, not an assortment of individual differences, which provides meaningful information about race.

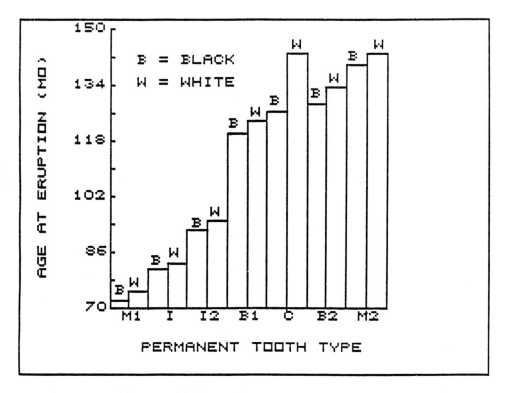

Figure 4. Age of Eruption of the Various Types of Permanent Teeth in Blacks and Whites.

Deciduous teeth were presented in Figure 3 with regard to the total number which had erupted per unit of age. Here, the mouths of Blacks and Whites were examined to determine the average age at which each permanent tooth type erupts. (I, B, C, and M indicate incisor, bicuspid, canine, and molar; 1 or 2 means first or second.) Both the upper and lower jaws were examined, but they produced the same results. Here, the upper jaw teeth are shown with the exception of the third molars, or wisdom teeth. The third molars are unstable and highly variable. Blacks lead Whites, on the average, for every permanent tooth. After the crossover in eruption rate of the baby teeth, Blacks develop the remaining baby teeth and each permanent tooth on an earlier schedule.

Thus far, the evidence which suggests that Blacks develop slower than either American Indians or Whites has been confined to birthweights and teeth. The studies on teeth and the observations on birthweights do verify each other, and they indicate that Blacks do develop slower. Whether or not teeth are indicative of total body development rate is problematic. However, a relatively recent line of evidence from finger ridge analysis strongly supports the research on birthweights and teeth. As of today, it offers the most compelling evidence for a slower early developmental period in Blacks.

Finger Ridge Development. The finger ridges are the raised lines on the tips of the fingers which form distinctive patterns. They are used to make fingerprints for identification. For several reasons, these ridges have proven to be one of the most useful features of humans for the study of early development. One, they are completely formed long before the child is born, so any unique finger ridge pattern must have originated when the baby was still inside the mother. Two, the finger ridges never change after they develop, so some insight into early development can be gained by looking at the fingerprints of adults, even of advanced age. Three, some features of finger ridges are under strong genetic control. Four, other features are extremely sensitive to environmental changes within the mother. Identical twins, having begun life as a single individual, should have identical fingerprints. Instead, slight variations of the environment inside the mother give rise to different finger ridge characteristics for each twin. Even Siamese twins have different fingerprints.

The finger ridges which are visible on the fingertips are called the *primary ridges*. Just beneath the skin there is one *secondary ridge* for each primary ridge. As it happens, when the finger ridges appear, all of the primary ridges develop first, then the secondary ridges begin to make their appearance. This phenomenon allows the investigator to formulate a sort of clock which tells how fast the ridges are developing in the unborn child. If there are fifteen primary ridges and five secondary ridges, development is 5/15 or ⅓ complete. By counting all the primary and secondary ridges, the researcher can determine which unborns are advanced and which are retarded in the development of finger ridges at a particular age.

Figure 5 graphically portrays the difference in ridge maturation time for Blacks and Whites. It is clear that the maturity of the finger ridges in Whites is advanced over that of Blacks. Retardation in the development of finger ridges is difficult to justify as anything other than an overall slower developmental rate. The number of ridges, the patterns they form, and how fast or slowly they develop are not germane to the subsequent welfare of the developing individual. In fact, there is no good reason why we should not all have exactly the same fingerprints, because one pattern works as well as another. Although complete absence of finger ridges is rare, the condition does occur, with no apparent impact on ability, life span, or fecundity.

Whether development of the finger ridges is indicative of the development of the baby as a whole still can be questioned. But three good lines of direct evidence—birthweights, teeth, and finger ridges—suggest that Blacks develop slower in the early stages, at least slower than American Indians and Whites. Aboriginally, the teeth comprised one of the most essential features of human beings; finger ridges may have been the least necessary. Thus, two features of Blacks—the least important and the most important—demonstrate a parallel growth and development rate. It seems likely that the rest of the body develops on the same schedule.

A further line of evidence having to do with the frequencies of birth defects shows that rapid development in Blacks—at least as indicated by birthweights—is not the desirable condition.

Birth Defects. Poverty, poor nutrition, lack of medical care, and other such socioeconomic disadvantages have all been blamed for the normally low birthweights among American Blacks. No doubt there is some truth in this view, perhaps a great deal. However, it is difficult to reconcile it with the incidence of birth defects among Blacks. It would be logical to assume that the impoverishment of Blacks not only causes them to be born smaller but also provokes a good chance of some malformation. Instead, American Whites are much more likely to suffer from common birth defects than are Blacks.

Rates of birth defects for Blacks and Whites have been intensively studied for three major systems of the body. These are the central nervous system, the respiratory system, and the heart and circulatory systems. Although the incidence of a defect in any of these systems is lower in Blacks for all the birthweights studied, Blacks tend to lose this advantage as the birthweights become greater. With regard to the central nervous system, over twice as many Whites as Blacks suffer defects if they are in the low birthweight category; if the birthweight is high, the ratio is five defective White newborns for every four defective Blacks. In defects of the respiratory system, there are about three-and-one-half Whites for every Black when the birthweight is at the minimum; at the highest

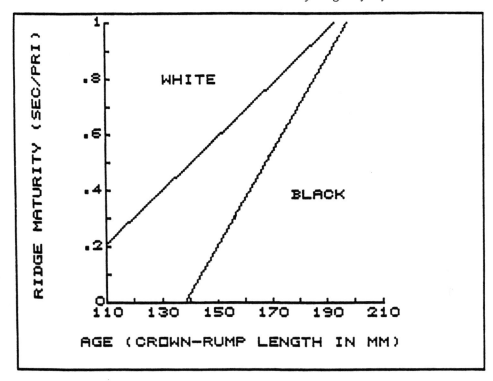

Figure 5. Maturity of the Finger Ridges in Unborn Black and White Babies of Different Ages.

The finger ridges which are used for making fingerprints are completely formed before the baby is born. During development their maturity can be gauged by counting the number of secondary ridges relative to the number of primary ridges, because the primaries are complete before the secondaries begin to develop. The straight line for each race is the one pathway which comes closest to all of the data points, which have been omitted for the sake of clarity. The plot demonstrates that the finger ridges of Whites mature on an earlier schedule than Blacks. This is probably the best evidence which argues for a slower early developmental period in Blacks.

birthweight, only one-and-one-third White newborns are affected for every Black. In the highest birthweight category for the heart and circulatory system, the number of affected Blacks and Whites is almost the same; in the lowest category, twice as many Whites as Blacks are afflicted. It is logical to assume that if average birthweights could be broken down into small increments, birth defects of Blacks in the highest weight categories would eventually surpass those in Whites. This is precisely what happens.

Birthweights have been broken down into rather narrow categories for three common birth defects. These are cleft palate, hypospadias, and anencephalus. Figure 6 shows the incidence of cleft palate for Blacks and

Whites in six birthweight categories. Whites suffer the highest incidence of the defect when the birthweight is the lowest. As the birthweight becomes progressively larger, the incidence declines. This would be the normal expectation if poverty is invoked for both low birthweights and a high frequency of birth defects. In this view, as the baby becomes "big and healthy," birth defects should decline. But Blacks do not fit in with this expectation. First, cleft palate is much less common in Blacks than in Whites, even at the lowest birthweight. Second, the defect becomes even less common at a low-medium birthweight. Third, contrary to expectation, the disorder becomes more frequent as the birthweight increases. At the highest birthweight, cleft palate is more frequent in Blacks than in Whites, and more frequent in the heaviest than in the lightest Black babies.

It is clear that something is going on here outside the realm of socioeconomics. If Blacks merely manifested a lower incidence of cleft palate overall, it might be explainable by speculating that the incidence today depends upon how many people with cleft palate survived in the past. Whites, with better medical care, and a more industrialized society, might have survived long enough with cleft palate to pass on their genes, thus increasing the probability that cleft palate would show up in the White population. However, the races are not merely different in overall frequency; they are of opposite polarity in the way that cleft palate is correlated with birthweight. In Whites, the incidence of the defect declines with an increase in birthweight; in Blacks, the incidence becomes greater. These results seem to say that "big" contradicts "healthy" in the birthweights of American Blacks.

Another common defect in males is in the penis. Normally, the penis is composed of three separate spongy cylinders which fuse during development. If these do not completely fuse, the penis is left with a hole or cleft somewhere along the shaft. This developmental error is known as hypospadias. Figure 7 shows the incidence of the condition for American Blacks and Whites of different birthweights.

The racial patterning of hypospadias with respect to birthweight looks very like that of cleft palate. Overall, Blacks suffer from the defect in far fewer numbers than do Whites. At the lowest birthweight, the condition can be seen in nearly three times as many Whites as Blacks. However, as birthweight increases, the frequency becomes greater in Blacks. Eventually, at the highest birthweight, more Blacks than Whites experience the anomaly. As in cleft palate, the incidence is lowest in Black babies of

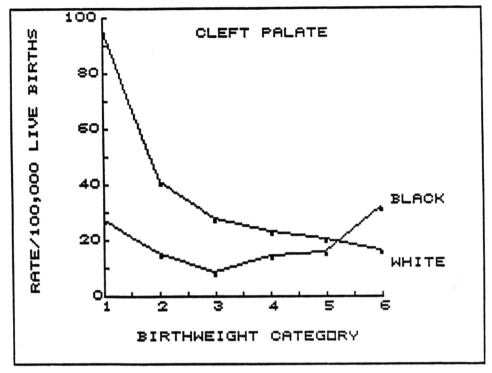

Figure 6. Incidence of Cleft Palate in Live Born Blacks and Whites.

Blacks develop with far fewer errors than do Whites, suggesting that slower, more certain development is normal in Blacks. The suggestion is even stronger when the incidence of each disorder is plotted against birthweight, as shown above for cleft palate. Categories 1 through 6 represent the following birthweights in grams:

    1, 2500 or less;   2, 2501–3000;   3, 3001–3500
    4, 3501–4000;   5, 4001–4500;   6, 4501 or more.

Blacks suffer the least rate of cleft palate if the birthweight is low to medium, and a greater rate as birthweight increases, eventually even surpassing the frequency in Whites. A loss of control in accuracy seems to be coupled with a control loss in size. Some process in Blacks evidently governs both the growth rate and the developmental trajectory.

a low-medium birthweight, and lowest in White babies of the highest birthweight.

It is unlikely that high birthweight itself is a cause of cleft palate or hypospadias in Blacks. Instead, there seems to be some sort of control mechanism which acts simultaneously on size and on the accuracy of the developmental trajectory. A low to medium birthweight appears to represent an optimal condition in Blacks. Both cleft palate and hypospadias show a characteristic bottoming out of frequency in these weight categories. In Whites, "the bigger the better" holds true; the frequencies of birth disorders drop as birthweight becomes progressively larger.

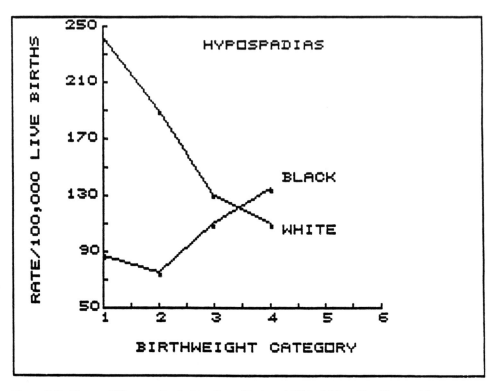

Figure 7. Incidence of Hypospadias in Live Born Black and White Males. (See Figure 6 for category weights.)

Hypospadias is a defect in the closure of the elements which form the penis. The error leaves a hole or cleft somewhere in the shaft. Compared to Whites, the incidence is quite low in Blacks. But once again, it is the low-medium birthweight category of Blacks which is most free from the defect. As birthweight increases to a maximum, so does the frequency of the developmental error. As in cleft palate, in the highest birthweight category Blacks exceed Whites in the number of defects. Like cleft palate, the frequency in Whites diminishes as birthweight increases. These data tend to verify a process in Blacks which controls both size and accuracy.

In anencephalus, shown in Figure 8, the brain fails to develop. The incidence of this error in Blacks markedly emphasizes an optimal birthweight for the race. Virtually unknown in Blacks in the low to medium birthweight categories, practically all the cases appear in newborns having the highest and lowest birthweights. In the highest birthweight category, the reported cases in Blacks outnumber defective Whites by a factor of nearly three to one. Still, the overall incidence is lower in Blacks than in Whites because of the extreme rarity of anencephalus in Black babies born in the optimal weight categories.

The three common birth defects discussed all point to a unique racial pattern with respect to birthweight, which differentiates Blacks from Whites. These anomalies are not, of course, the only developmental errors which can occur, but they are among the most common. Their incidences support the racial patterning of the defects in the central nervous system, the respiratory system, and the heart and circulatory system.

The present rate of the developmental errors is probably reflective of the incidence which predominated in the past. It is highly doubtful that any of the three errors could be survived under living conditions outside of advanced civilization. Certainly, anencephalus cannot be survived under any conditions. In cleft palate, food and accompanying microorganisms tend to become lodged in the nasopharynx, and consequent lethal infection is likely. In hypospadias, the penis can be easily invaded by bacteria. Effective surgical treatment for cleft palate and hypospadias has been available only in the past few decades, a time much too short to cause an appreciable increase in the frequency of the defects.

Finger Ridges, Miscarriages, and Abortions. The old adage of the "big and healthy" baby doesn't hold up in the case of Blacks. An additional line of evidence involving the maturation of finger ridges in miscarriages and abortions emphasizes that the terms "fast-growing" and "healthy" aren't very good companions in Blacks either. The difference between normal Black and White unborns in the maturation of the finger ridges has been presented earlier. The ridges of Blacks mature later than those of Whites. A later rate of ridge maturation can be looked at as one indication that Blacks normally develop slower than Whites overall. It is instructive to compare the maturation rates in cases of miscarriage to the rate in cases of abortion within each of the two races.

For comparative purposes miscarried unborns can be considered as developmental failures and abortuses can be regarded as normal babies. Babies that have been miscarried, sometimes called "spontaneous abortions," do not survive the full term. These are distinguished here from "elective abortions," which presumably would have survived. The less cumbersome terms "miscarriage" and "abortion" are employed here.

More babies are miscarried early in the pregnancy than later. Exactly why a miscarriage occurs is often unknown, but it is assumed to be a result of some developmental flaw in the baby or some incompetence in the biology of the mother. Whether the maternal system destroys the

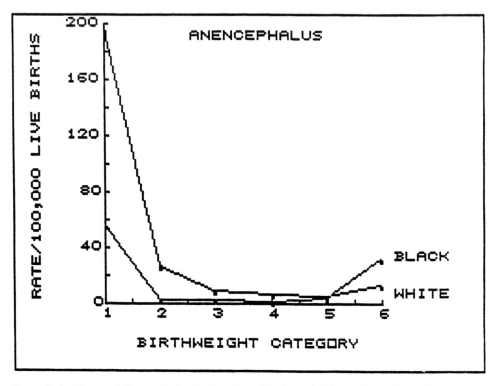

Figure 8. Incidence of Anencephalus in Live Born Blacks and Whites. (See Fig. 6 for category weights.)

Failure of the brain to develop is called anencephalus. The brain is one of the first structures to form, thus anencephalus is an error which occurs early in development. It is notable that nearly all cases in Blacks occur in the lightest or heaviest birthweight categories. The line for Blacks has the characteristic dip in the middle, as it does in cleft palate and hypospadias, but here the dip reaches a near-zero level for all intermediate birthweight categories. This supports the idea of a control process in Blacks which operates on both accuracy and growth rate. In Whites, the defect is most prevalent in the lowest birthweight category. Like cleft palate and hypospadias, anencephalus occurs more frequently in Blacks than Whites in the heaviest birthweight category.

fetus or the fetus self-destructs is not known. In any case, the pregnancy can be thought of as a maternal/fetus system which fails to bring the offspring to fruition. The reason for the failure seems to be detected internally by the system itself soon after conception. Many more miscarriages occur than is generally acknowledged, and some investigators have estimated that as many as 30 percent of all pregnancies end in miscarriage. Most of these are believed to occur so soon after conception that the mother is unaware of it. It is possible that the process responsible for destroying a malformed fetus is built into the system. If this is true, the birth of an infant with a non-survivable defect may be an indication that the destructive process failed to operate properly early in the pregnancy.

In an abortion, intentional outside interference with the maternal/fetus system has terminated the pregnancy for one non-medical reason or another. It is logical to assume that if such interference had not occurred, the pregnancy would have resulted in a normal offspring.

Figure 9 shows a comparison of finger ridge maturation rates in White miscarriages and White abortions. The maturation rates are about what would be expected. The miscarriages fail to develop finger ridges as rapidly as do the normal White babies. Intuitively, this would seem to be the logical pattern. If something goes wrong with the maternal/fetus system, development slows down, eventually stops, and a miscarriage ensues. Retardation in finger ridge maturation comes as no surprise, nor would it be unexpected to learn that major organs and systems had failed to develop.

The difference in finger ridge maturation rate of miscarried and aborted Blacks is directly opposed to Whites. Figure 10 illustrates that a Black developmental failure is more advanced in ridge maturity than is the normal Black unborn! Rapidly maturing ridges, and the fact that the child has been miscarried, points to some sort of speed or timing control that has been lost in the developmental process. Carrying this supposition further, in the light of the previous information on birth defects, had the baby not been miscarried, he or she would have developed rapidly, have been large at birth, and would have been born with a high probability of being afflicted with a birth defect. Instead, some internal process might have signalled the outcome, and the pregnancy was spontaneously terminated by the maternal/fetal system.

Again, here is another example of Blacks demonstrating the exact reverse of Whites in the developmental process. From research on teeth and finger ridges, Whites appear to develop rapidly, while Blacks seem to develop slowly. Birth defects are frequent in small White babies and large Black babies. Miscarried Whites are retarded in finger ridge maturity; miscarried Blacks are advanced. The explanation which makes the most sense from these observations is that the development of Blacks is a slower, more carefully controlled process.

It should be apparent at this point that the lower birthweight in Blacks probably is not merely a result of poverty. Although low socioeconomic status may account for a large component of low birthweights, the total

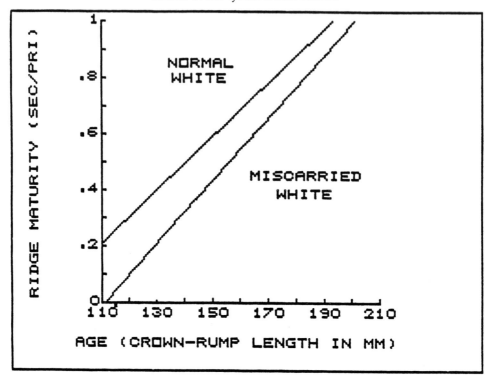

Figure 9. Maturity of the Finger Ridges in Normal and Miscarried Whites of Different Ages.

The difference in maturation of the finger ridges between normal and miscarried Whites is about what would be expected. The finger ridges fail to mature in the miscarried babies as rapidly as they do normally. Although raw data points are not shown, there is virtually no overlap between the two groups. Nearly all the data points which direct the White normal line are to the left of the miscarriage line. Intuitively, this result seems logical because developmental retardation would be expected in cases of miscarriage, where failure of the maternal/fetal system has culminated in the spontaneous termination of the pregnancy.

picture is more complex. Racial differences must also play a significant role. These differences have been accumulating for thousands of years. Redistribution of present-day resources, as desirable as it might be socially, will be of no consequence to the racial effect, at least not anytime soon.

Birthweights and Tobacco Toxins. If a process in Blacks operates to keep the developing child relatively small and free of defects, it is reasonable to assume that the same process would help protect the developing infant from harmful influences introduced from the environment. Although not conducted to test this assumption, one area of research does argue for a buffering mechanism in Blacks that operates more efficiently if the birthweight is low or medium than if it is large. In Whites, the buffer operates about the same no matter what the birthweight.

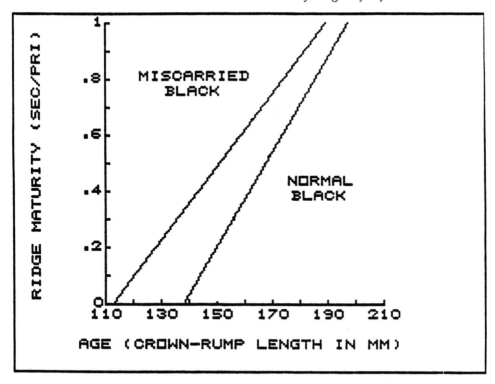

Figure 10. Maturity of the Finger Ridges in Normal and Miscarried Blacks of Different Ages.

The results shown in this plot can be contrasted to those of Whites in the previous figure. Black miscarriages are diametrically opposite White miscarriages. Instead of being retarded in the maturation of the finger ridges, Black miscarriages are advanced over the normally developing Black fetuses. These results elegantly suggest that a rapidly developing Black fetus represents the abnormal condition. There is very little overlap between the two groups of Blacks, nearly all of the data points which direct the miscarriage line being to the left of data points for normally developing infants. Raw data points are not shown.

The existence of such a buffer can be hypothesized from the results of studies on the effects of cigarette smoking. It is well established that smoking cigarettes on the part of the mother will, on the average, reduce the birthweight of her baby no matter what her racial affinity happens to be. The question posed here is: does a racial difference exist in the degree that the baby is affected? If so, is the effect the same on all size babies?

The information available consists of a number of smoking and non-smoking Black and White mothers of various prepregnancy weights and the birthweights of their babies. It has already been shown that the birthweight of a baby is highly correlated with the mother's normal weight. More often than not, a large mother and a large baby go hand in hand. Figure 11 demonstrates that in Whites, the toxins in cigarette smoke produce a more or less systematic effect on birthweight. The correlation between the normal weights of the mothers and the birthweights of their babies is about the same in both the smoking and non-smoking groups of Whites. A large White mother who smokes tends to have a large baby compared to other White smokers but not as large as the non-smoker of her own weight. The only difference among Whites is that babies born to smokers are smaller than babies of the non-smokers. The baby's weight deficit is about the same no matter what the mother's normal prepregnancy weight.

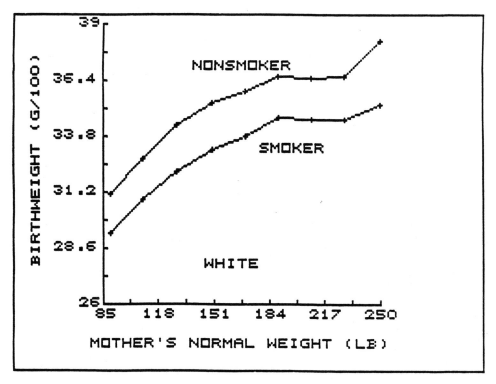

Figure 11. Difference in Birthweights Between Smoking and Nonsmoking White Mothers of Various Prepregnancy Weights.

The nonsmoker line plotted above is identical to the line for White mothers shown in Figure 1. The nonsmoker and smoker lines demonstrate that babies born of mothers who use tobacco average a consistently smaller birthweight than babies of mothers who do not smoke. In spite of the smaller birthweights, the weight of the White smoker's baby at birth maintains the same degree of correlation with the mother's normal prepregnancy weight. This is shown by the parallel nature of the two lines. In Whites, the use of tobacco seems to cause a generalized loss of weight in the developing infant across all the prepregnancy weights of the mothers.

In Blacks, the situation is not so simple. As is evident in Figure 12, toxins from tobacco have less effect on the birthweight of the baby in the low and medium prepregnancy weight groups. As the normal weight of the mother increases beyond the medium, the Black baby suffers a proportionately greater weight loss from the effects of tobacco. In addition, the baby's weight loses its correlation with the mother's normal prepregnancy weight. Above a prepregnancy weight of about 175 pounds, where smoking exerts a minimal effect on birthweights, the average weight of a group of Black babies can no longer be predicted from their mothers' average prepregnancy weights. Instead, the birthweights fluctuate.

It is clear that the effect on the birthweights of babies whose mothers smoke is systematic in Whites. In Blacks, the effect is less and systematic only up to a certain point. These results go along with the hypothesized developmental control mechanism in Blacks. At low to medium birthweights, the baby has been well protected from the effects of cigarette smoke. At high birthweights, control has been lost or degraded somewhere along the developmental line, and the loss has left the baby more open to the toxic effects of tobacco.

Stated in terms of total size of the maternal/fetal unit, the small Black unit does a better job of warding off the effects of tobacco toxins than does the large Black unit. In Whites, the ability to buffer the effects of tobacco is about the same no matter what the size of the unit. Thus, the specific effect of size is not the same in both races. These results suggest the existence of a size threshold in Blacks which, when exceeded, represents an abnormality for the race. Such a threshold seems to fit the information presented earlier. A high rate of developmental errors and a reduced ability to buffer tobacco toxins are characteristic of the large Black baby.

Summary of Early Development. This section began with the question of whether or not Blacks are supposed to be smaller at birth than the babies of other races. The studies which have been conducted do not answer that question once and for all times. Nevertheless, the cumulative impact of all the foregoing research should instill some strong suspicion that developmental rates and birthweights are naturally lower in American Blacks. As the babies of each race develop along toward a common date of birth, the tooth buds of Blacks are smaller than those of American Indians, and the finger ridges of Blacks are less mature than those of Whites. On the date of birth, Black babies are smaller than babies of the other two races. In the first two years of breathing life, Blacks erupt fewer

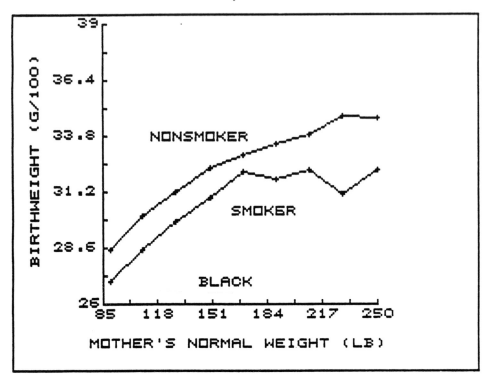

Figure 12. Difference in Birthweights Between Smoking and Nonsmoking Black Mothers of Various Prepregnancy Weights.

The lines plotted in this figure for babies of nonsmoking and smoking Black mothers can be contrasted with the lines plotted for White mothers, shown in the previous figure. There is less difference in the birthweights of Black babies born to smoking and nonsmoking mothers, but only up to a certain prepregnancy weight. Above that weight, the birthweight of the Black baby loses its close correlation with the mother's normal weight, and birthweight differences between smokers and nonsmokers is greater than in Whites. The smaller Black baby appears to be more protected from the effects of tobacco toxins than is the heavier baby.

teeth than Whites. Suddenly, at about two years of age, Blacks begin to erupt teeth faster than Whites. Blacks also grow a bit taller than Whites up to the time of puberty, as will be discussed later.

Slow development and a small birthweight seem to be the desirable conditions for Blacks. A miscarried Black has faster-maturing finger ridges than a normal Black baby. A Black baby of large birthweight is more prone to birth defects than a smaller Black baby. If Black mothers smoke cigarettes, the effects are greater on the large baby than on the small.

Exactly how this seeming slowdown would be incorporated in the developmental process is difficult to specify. It would be naive to assume that it is simply an overall slackening of pace in each biological process.

It would also demonstrate inexperience to expect that it is a specialized function peculiar to Blacks. More likely, it is some sort of complex timing mechanism which operates more intensely in Blacks because its operation has been relaxed to some degree in other races.

However it may operate, the idea of a slow, more certain developmental period explains a number of other observations which are not definitive enough to achieve the status of racial features. For example, the third molars, or "wisdom teeth," are unstable in all modern people. They are absent in 20 percent of the American White population but in only 10 percent of American Blacks. Also, reported correlations among the sizes of paired structures are higher in Blacks than in Whites, suggesting that the developmental process in Blacks is better able to produce the same individual on both sides of the midline of the body. Based upon observations such as these, it seems probable that other, yet to be accomplished studies will produce similar results. For example, a muscle in the forearm, the palmaris longus, is absent in a significant number of people. Based upon the presence of a slow, certain developmental period in Blacks, it would be my guess that the muscle will prove to be absent in fewer Blacks than Whites. This, of course, awaits to be determined. But the concept of slow and accurate development as a racial feature of Blacks permits the formulation of some specific expectations for future testing. The concept is tantalyzing to the anthropologist, because it is easy to explain in anthropological terms. The racial feature might have come into being as an adaptive mechanism. If so, such a trait would have a neat connection with the efficient use of energy in Subsaharan Africa. This possible connection is explored later in Chapter 6.

4

BLACK PHYSICAL FEATURES
IN YOUTH AND ADULTHOOD

Introduction. To the anthropologist, races are a dynamic manifestation of many forces. The ultimate force causing their formation is the environment, because it dictates what we wear, what we breathe, and what plants and animals we must kill to eat. In response, individual members of a group or race live long or short lives, producing many or few offspring, depending upon their fitness. Over a long period of time, fitness levels prescribe what genes will accumulate in the race or group. Fitness, of course, refers to the ability to reproduce. It has no direct link with virtues such as strength, courage, and the like. As ruthless as this weeding-out process seems to be from an individual's viewpoint, it is aimed at group survival through time. The genetic structure of a group can be considered as a sort of conservation measure which ensures that each generation does not have to start from scratch in adapting to the conditions of a particular area. Genes, and particular combinations of genes, perpetuate the physical features which already have proven to be desirable. Fortunately, the process is neither exact nor all-inclusive. Any group of humans is marked by rather extreme biological variation among many of its members. This condition acts as insurance against short-term catastrophic events. To illustrate, if all females in a group were highly similar, then a disease which could kill one female might well kill them all.

Many racial features have no good explanation at this time as to how they originated. It would be wonderful if a few archaic human beings remained behind to show how far each of the races has departed from the original model. But no such standard exists, so there is no way of telling if the skin of Blacks became dark, having been light in the ancient ancestors, or if the skin of Whites was formerly dark. It can be argued that West Europeans gradually lost their skin coloration to enhance the absorption of reduced ultraviolet radiation. Likewise, one might speculate that Blacks developed deep skin coloration to protect them from an overabundance of the sun's rays, or as protective coloration in jungle shadows. The lips of Whites might have become reduced and more inverted as an adaptation to cold, or the process might have been reversed in Blacks to help withstand the tropical heat. One can in fact argue on and on about the origin of many racial features with no real factual return. Someday these problems will be solved. But today, most of the adult racial features presented in this chapter fall into the mystery category.

In the previous chapter, racial features were confined to biological processes in early development. The important Black feature was described as a slow, accurate development phase which culminates in offspring who are relatively free of developmental errors. The Black youth and adult racial features presented here are mostly related to bone and bony structures. There is a good reason why. Bones and teeth remain intact long after the softer tissues decompose. The bones which remain after violent or accidental death are often the only clue to the age, race, sex, and identity of the individual victim. The forensic specialist must provide such information, based on traits related to bone. Bones sometimes petrify and thereby persist through time. Thus, historically, anthropologists have based the classification of humans on the characters of bone. The size and shape of an individual is largely determined by bone, which in turn owes a great deal to genetic heritage. The covering tissues such as muscle and fat may be mostly molded by an outside force such as occupation. In fact, a multibillion-dollar industry in America subsists soley on our desire to change our fat and muscle components, to darken or lighten our skins, and to straighten or curl our hair, in spite of our genetic heritage. However, bone is also somewhat of a plastic tissue. The bones of a starving child will not grow as large as a well-nourished one. The skull can be shaped by chewing and sleeping habits, as well as by intentional deformation, a fairly extensive practice among certain societies. In spite of these environmental effects, bone size and shape more closely reflects real racial features better than do traits of soft tissue, which can result mostly from a peculiar diet, exercise, or other force of the immediate environment.

Youth Stature and Body Proportion. Figure 13 compares the heights of Black, Mexican-American, and White children from two years of age to the age of seventeen. There is virtually no difference in the average height between Black and White adults, but children do exhibit some differences. Mexican-Americans are shorter than their Black and White counterparts, both as children and as adults. After the crossover in tooth maturation rate occurs at about two years of age, Black children tend to be slightly taller than White children, and this difference persists up to the age of puberty. Following adolescence, Whites are as tall as Blacks. In the growth phase, there isn't a tremendous amount of difference among the three groups, but Mexican-Americans reach their maximum heights sooner than either Blacks or Whites.

Stature is a highly composite measure which hides a great deal of variability. Two professional fighters may be the same height and weight, but in the flesh, their body features may not even vaguely resemble each other. The same is true with respect to race. There are significant racial differences in the proportions of body parts which go to make up total height. Figures 14 and 15 show leg lengths and sitting heights for Black, Mexican-American, and White children for the ages from two to seventeen years. In these features, Blacks are completely in a class of their own, both as adults and throughout the growth period. The racial differences are clear with regard to Blacks, less clear between Mexican-Americans and Whites. The legs of Blacks are longer, and their torsos are shorter than the other two groups, both relative to height and in an absolute sense. After puberty, White torsos are longer than Mexican-Americans; Whites have somewhat longer legs than Mexican-Americans throughout the growth period but not so emphatically as do Blacks.

The longer legs and different proportions have been reported in Blacks even before birth. There can be no doubt that the features are truly racial traits. Apparently, the same cannot be said for these features in all races. In modern times, Orientals, especially the Japanese, have undergone a dramatic increase in stature. Nearly all the increase in height has come from a lengthening of the legs, the torso hardly being affected at all. Although the ultimate cause of this stature increase is unknown, the fact that it has been confined to the legs is highly suggestive of a post-war enhancement of nutrition during childhood. Leg growth tends to get the short end of the stick under conditions of inadequate diet. Better dietary elements have permitted individuals to come closer to reaching their genetic potential in leg length. This seems to be a clear case of a difference in the immediate environment instead of a racial difference ultimately imparted by long-term differences in climate.

Adult Stature and Leg Bone Proportions. To most people, the word "leg" and "arm" do not mean the same thing as they do to the anatomist or physical anthropologist. Technically, there are the upper limbs and

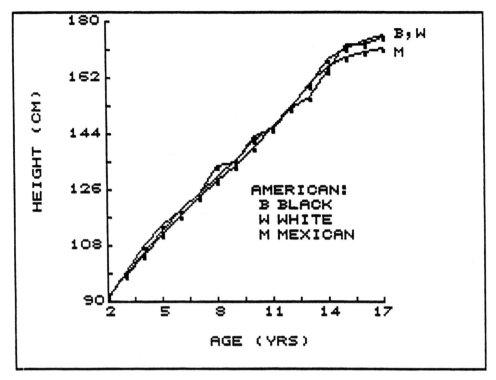

Figure 13. Heights of American Black, Mexican, and White Children Aged Two to Seventeen Years.

American Blacks are somewhat taller, on the average, than either Mexican-Americans or Whites up to the age of puberty. Following puberty, Blacks and Whites are equal in height and Mexican-Americans are shorter. Apparently these statures are reflective of the genetic structure for each group, because the children are on similar diets and live under similar conditions in the United States. There is no difference in stature between adult West African Blacks and West European Whites, so the transplant of those people to the New World has had no effect on their relative heights.

the lower limbs. The upper limb is composed of the arm, the forearm, the wrist, and the hand. The lower limb is composed of the thigh, the leg, the ankle, and the foot. So "arm" is technically the first segment of the upper limb, and "leg" is the second segment of the lower limb. Here, the common usages of the words "leg" and "arm" are employed and refer to the entire lower and upper limb, respectively. "Upper arm" and "lower leg" refer to the obvious specific segments of each limb.

Figure 16 shows the most conservative estimate available for the contribution of leg lengths to total adult body height. As Figure 16 demonstrates, the length of the torso in adult Blacks does not contribute as much to stature as it does in Whites. The percentages shown include the length of the foot. If the foot is not included, as it is not in the previous informa-

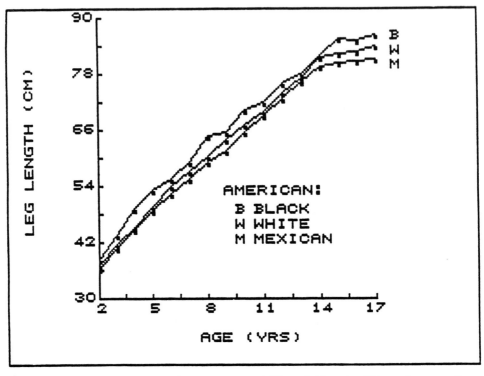

Figure 14. Leg Lengths of American Black, Mexican, and White Children Aged Two to Seventeen Years.

The upper and lower limbs of American Blacks are longer than the other two groups even in the fetal stage. Blacks maintain these longer limbs all the way through childhood and adulthood. Here the leg lengths are compared among the three groups. Blacks are distinctly separate from the other groups at the start, while Whites and Mexican-Americans are nearly equal at two years of age. As growth progresses, White legs become distinctly longer than the legs of Mexican-Americans. In the past, a common racial slur was a comparison of Black body proportions to those of the great ape. Here, it is obvious that both Whites and Mexican-Americans resemble apes more than Blacks by having shorter legs relative to overall height.

tion on Blacks, Mexican-Americans, and Whites, the percentages of total height which the legs contribute are 47.25, 47.72, and 49.92 percent for Mexican-American, White, and Black seventeen-year-olds, respectively. Whites and Mexican-Americans differ by less than one-half of 1 percent, while Blacks and Whites differ by over 1½ percent. Blacks differ from Mexican-Americans by over 2½ percent. For differences based on averages, these are quite large.

One notion in the older literature is that limb length is an adaptation to the predators of an area. The proposition was that Africans needed short bursts of speed to avoid being eaten by a lion. Thus, longer legs became more frequent in Blacks, because Blacks who had them in the

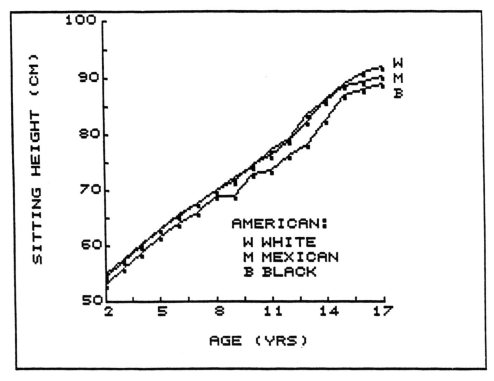

Figure 15. Sitting Heights of American Black, Mexican, and White Children Aged Two to Seventeen Years.

Sitting height is exactly what it implies, the height from the chair seat to the top of the head. The variability in sitting height is primarily a difference in torso length, but head and neck differences play some part. Blacks are distinctly separate from the other two groups at the start. The difference between Whites and Mexican-Americans is most patent after puberty. The longer legs and shorter torsos of Blacks result in a total stature which does not differ from Whites in adulthood. The portion of total height contributed by sitting height in the adult is about fifty-three percent in Mexican-Americans, fifty-two percent in Whites, and fifty percent in Blacks.

past were able to escape and to pass on their genes for longer legs to each succeeding generation. This speculative venture now seems rather far-fetched, but it cannot be totally discounted. For one thing, it is now known that predators don't eat all that much prey compared to the reproductive capacity of the prey group. It would be counterproductive to the livelihood of predators to eat so much that the population of the prey group was significantly affected. For another, it is now known that most predators prey upon either immature animals, who do not rely on speed for escape, or the old and handicapped, who are not likely to pass on many genes anyway.

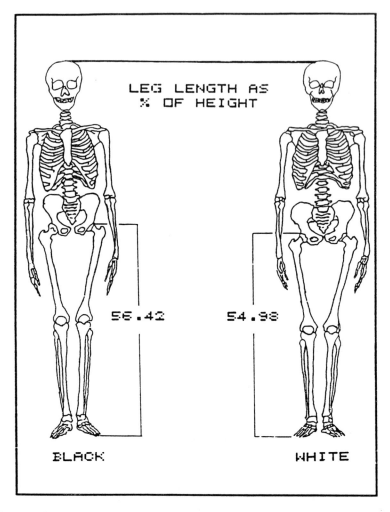

Figure 16. Proportion of Stature Provided by the Legs in American Blacks and Whites.

However the racial feature got started, it must have been quite important in an adaptive sense. It may be that the characteristic is an adaptive response to climate. The limbs and the torso can be considered as cylinders of various volumes. A long cylinder has more outside surface than a short one of the same volume (discounting the top and bottom areas), so there ends up being more area of skin in Blacks per unit of body volume. The resultant is a more efficient cooling mechanism in Blacks and a more efficient heat-retention mechanism in Whites. Thermal regulation may be the major force behind this racial difference. This hypothesis is inherently more attractive than the predator theory, because, in general, mammals follow along the same line. In northern latitudes, they tend to be chunky and short-limbed, and become more linear and long-limbed toward the equator.

Blacks and Whites also differ in the proportions of the leg itself. For the same leg length, the contributions of thigh and lower leg tend to be more equal in Blacks. Figure 17 presents a comparison of leg proportions between Blacks and Whites. The foot contributes the same amount in both races. Whites have longer thighs and shorter lower legs when compared to the shorter thighs and longer lower legs of Blacks.

A number of popular authors, Norman Mailer among them, have observed that Blacks, especially males, have a more graceful walk than

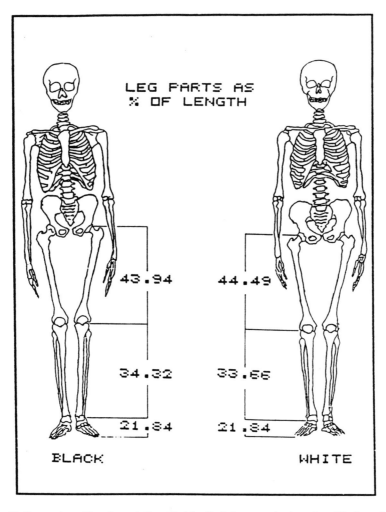

Figure 17. Proportion of Leg Length Provided by Each Segment in American Blacks and Whites.

Whites. Mailer used the cat's prowl to describe the walk of Blacks, and the bear's swaying gait to the locomotion of Whites. If this is a valid observation, whether scientifically described or not, it may have more to do with racial features than with learned behavior. However, human locomotion is extremely complex, involving the interplay of at least hundreds of elements, and is in fact a specialty field within the profession of physical anthropology itself. Research so fine-grained to expose racial differences in locomotion has not yet been conducted, nor is it likely to be in the forseeable future. Nevertheless, it is tempting to speculate on the possibility that more equal right and left halves of the body, and more equal lengths of each leg segment, contribute to a smoother walk in Blacks. In short, the possibility is speculative, but it is not entirely hogwash.

The long bones of the leg are frequently used to make stature estimates of individuals. Blacks and Whites are sufficiently different to require separate tables of reference for such estimates. If racial affinity is not correctly assessed beforehand, considerable error in stature estimates can result. If the leg bones are measured and the White table is used to estimate the height of a Black, the calculated stature is greater than the actual height. The reverse is also true: the Black long bone table producing a lesser height for Whites than is the actual case.

Adult Stature and Arm Bone Proportions. The lengths of the upper and lower limbs are positively correlated. More times than not, people with long legs also have long arms. Figure 18 shows a comparison of Blacks and Whites in arm length and stature. Blacks have longer arms than Whites, both relative to total height and in an absolute sense. This is an everyday observation even to the unkeen eye. In telecasts of professional fights, it is rare when the reach of a White boxer exceeds that of his Black opponent in the same weight class.

Figure 19 demonstrates the racial differences in arm proportions. Distribution of the upper-limb segments are almost exactly correlated with that of the lower limb. Blacks have a more equitable distribution in the lengths of upper arm, forearm, and hand. In comparison, Whites have longer upper arms and shorter forearms. Unlike the feet, the hands of Whites are shorter than those of Blacks. Both the arm length and the arm proportions in Blacks are different from Whites before birth. As is the case with the legs, the arm features are truly under genetic control.

Once again, it should be emphasized that a great deal of overlap exists between the races. Blacks with long torsos and short legs, Whites with short

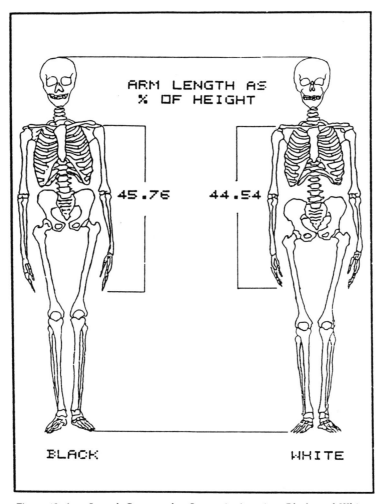

ARM LENGTH AS
% OF HEIGHT

45.76   44.54

BLACK   WHITE

Figure 18. Arm Length Compared to Stature in American Blacks and Whites.

torsos and long legs, and all combinations in between are not rare. Only by looking at large numbers of people can it be ascertained that Blacks differ from Whites in average leg lengths, limb proportions, and limb length/stature ratios.

The reader may wonder how the forensic anthropologist can examine bones and provide an accurate assessment of race if so much overlap exists among the races. The answer is that he or she must look at a number of simultaneous measurements and traits. For example, one ratio may have a forty–sixty chance of not being from a Black bone. If another ratio has the same odds, the probability of both characters being in a bone that is not Black is only about two in five. Find another ratio, and the odds that the bone is not from a Black individual are only about one in three. As features more typical of Blacks accumulate in one skeleton, the probability of the skeleton not being from a Black person can become very low. Race assessment from bones never, of course, reaches absolute certainty, but the probability of being correct can be quite high if enough bones are available for examination.

Skull Features. Of all the bones, the skull is the most important in racial classification. Technically, the word "skull" is a collective reference for all of the assembled bones of the head. Removing the mandible, or lower jaw, leaves the cranium, destroying the face leaves the calvarium,

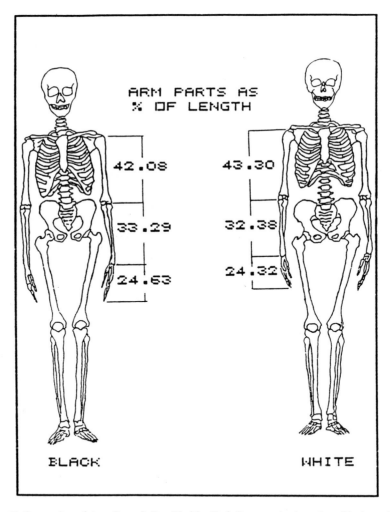

Figure 19. Proportion of Arm Length Provided by Each Segment in American Blacks and Whites.

and breaking away the bony base of the calvarium leaves the calva. The calva is often the last part which remains after the rest of the skull has deteriorated. This technically correct nomenclature is now somewhat confounded in anthropological literature. The terms "skull" and "cranium" are often used interchangeably; "cranial capacity" has always been used instead of "calvarial capacity" to refer to the space allotted to the brain and its supporting structures. "Braincase" or "brainpan" sometimes supplants the term "calvarium," and most investigators would not be offended if somebody included under "craniometric features" the measurements of the lower jaw. The reader should not be surprised if the terminology used here does not coincide exactly with that of other references.

Figure 20 presents some of the more obvious racial features of the skull. Compared to Whites, the lower face projects forward in Blacks. The bony entrance around the nose is smoother in Blacks than in Whites, the eye sockets in Blacks are more square or rectangular than round. The forehead is more straight up and down, and the bony ridges over the brow are smaller than the typical receding forehead and heavy brow ridges of Whites. In Blacks, the back of the skull forms the shape of a bun in profile, the calva being the top slice, the base being the lower slice. It has been my personal observation that in profiles of living individuals, the neck and the back of the head frequently form a straight line in Blacks, while Whites more often than not exhibit a question mark shape. However, this may reflect a difference in the muscularity of the neck, since this feature has been observed mostly in professional athletes. The mastoid processes, the bony protrusions below the ear canals, are generally shorter and less robust in Blacks. Overall, the White skull presents a more rugged and variable terrain. The Black skull is smoother and more graceful. Figure 21 is a frontal view of the cranium. It shows the tendency of the Black calva to be low and the bone between the eye sockets to be wide. In Blacks, the bony root of the nose is a smooth elevation, rounded from side-to-side like the roof of an underpass. Whites have somewhat of an arch at the peak of the calva, and the bone between the eye sockets is comparatively narrow. The nose root is higher in elevation and shaped like a levee topped by a narrow road. When the head is turned slowly from a frontal to a profile position, soon only one eye can be seen in Whites because of the elevated root of the nose. In Blacks, both eyes are visible longer, and it is not rare for both eyes to appear in profile.

What these features mean is not clear. Skulls of the human predecessors of both Blacks and Whites, the so-called "cavemen" or Neanderthals, have features of both races, such as the bun-shaped calvarium evident in modern Blacks, and the receding forehead and heavy brow ridges often seen in Whites today, especially males. One feature, the nasal opening, can be explained by vapor pressure. The maximum width of the nasal opening divided by its length is called the nasal index. A long, narrow nose has a lower nasal index than a short, broad nose. This index is almost perfectly correlated with the average vapor pressure of water, which in turn is a good indicator of mean annual temperature. Inhabitants of the hotter and more humid climates typical of low latitudes and low elevations, have a higher nasal index than do the natives of cooler

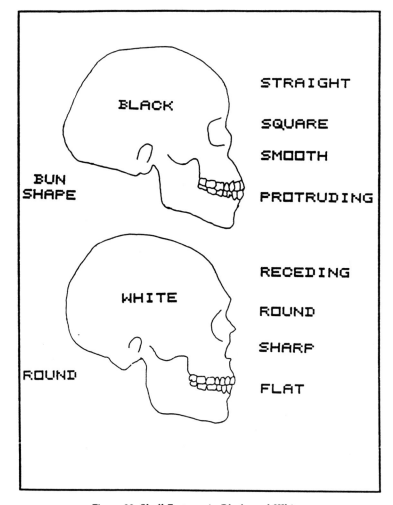

Figure 20. Skull Features in Blacks and Whites.

and drier areas. Some of the other differences in skull features between Blacks and Whites may have to do with the nasal index. It is important to remember that the skull is a highly complicated and integrated structure and not just a bony protection for the brain. A change in the nasal index may require a change in the shape of the calvarium to accommodate it. Since the muscles used in chewing originate on the calvarium, a change in its shape may require reconstruction of the lower jaw. In short, it is possible that alteration of major portions of the skull may be necessary to incorporate a functional emphasis in only one part of it.

Relative to the calvarium, in which the brain is lodged, the facial bones are frequently more massive in Blacks, making the calvarium

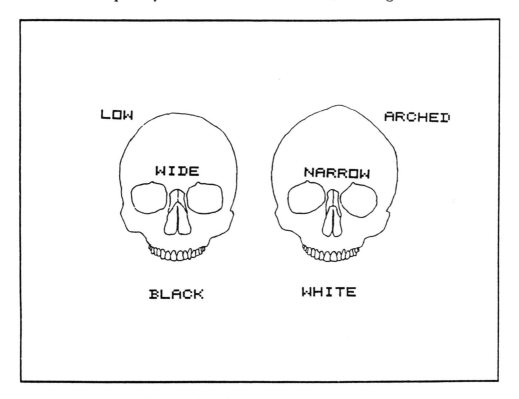

Figure 21. Cranial Features in Blacks and Whites.

This frontal view of the cranium shows the tendency of the eye sockets to be rectangular in Blacks, round in Whites. The top of the cranium, the calva, is low in Blacks, arched in Whites. Both the nasal opening and the bony bridge between the eye sockets are wide in Blacks. The nasal bones forming the root of the nose are low and rounded in Blacks, high and sharper in Whites. Although not shown in this view, the front teeth of Blacks are larger than Whites, and the muzzle projects forward to a greater degree. Overall, the White cranium appears more rugged, with emphasized peaks and valleys; the Black cranium is smoother.

appear to have a small capacity. Boxing great and former heavyweight champion Larry Holmes appears to have a small cranial capacity because of his robust facial construction. In reality, no difference in brain volume exists between Blacks and Whites. Mongoloids have a slightly greater brain volume than either Blacks or Whites, and Neanderthals, or "cavemen," had substantially larger brains than humans do today. Fortunately, brain size seems to have little to do with intellectual capacity. The smallest brain on record, about two-thirds the size of the modern average, is the one which belonged to French novelist Anatole France.

In spite of the differences in skull morphology outlined above, seldom does an individual skull present all Black or all White features. Instead, the features overlap to a considerable extent. Given a skull and no other information except that it is either American Black or White, anthropologists sometimes classify it Black when it is really from a White, and vice versa. The overlap among races is evident in skull shape as well as virtually every other racial feature. Nevertheless, with enough measurements and sufficient features available, the probability of an intact skull being misclassified is only about one out of twenty if it is examined by a professional anthropologist. The important point is that racial assessment is a painstaking process, and anybody who has finally become proficient at it soon comes to mistrust a person who merely looks over a skull and pronounces it "Negro," or whatever, on the basis of one or two features. The process requires measurements using special instruments, advanced statistical techniques, study of topographic features, and often a sort of "feel" gained from years of experience.

Head Hardness and Body Density. Athletic organizations keep tables of numbers by which body density can be estimated from skinfold measurements. To make a skinfold measurement, the investigator pinches the skin on various parts of the body, measures the thickness of each fold, and refers to established tables to determine the subject's total body fat and body density. There is enough difference between Blacks and Whites that separate tables of numbers are required for the two races. Blacks have a higher percentage of lean body mass than do Whites. Even if the White and Black subjects are both pudgy, Blacks tend to have a more dense body. A denser body is, of course, another way of saying a heavier weight for the same volume.

There is no doubt that the skeleton contributes a substantial amount to the high density in the bodies of Blacks. Figure 22 shows the difference in Black and White bone density for the lower back vertebrae and the femurs, or thigh bones, for both males and females. The Black male has the densest bones, the White male and Black female are approximately equal in bone density, and the White female has the least dense bones. There is no reason to believe that the other bones of the body do not follow the same pattern. Forensic anthropologists, accustomed to close scrutiny of bone for keys to racial affinity, often remark on a grayish, marmoreal quality of the Black cranium, especially the calva, but this feature has not been quantified or made explicit in the literature. Presumably, this is a characteristic imparted by the greater density of the Black skull.

Density is sometimes confused with hardness, because the two are often related. Still, they are not the same quality. Gold is much more dense than iron, but not nearly as hard. In bone, the two qualities are bound up together, because it is the mineralization of bone which imparts virtually all of the hardness and most of the density. A long bone minus its minerals is light and so soft that it can be tied into a knot. The skeletons of Blacks, being more intensely mineralized, are both more hard and more dense than the skeletons of Whites.

The body density of Blacks results in negative buoyancy in many individual cases. The body tends to sink in water instead of floating to the surface. A high proportion of lean body mass is not desirable in the competitive swimmer, and this may be one reason that few Blacks are involved in the sport. There are, of course, numerous other possible reasons more associated with socioeconomic status than biology. Among these are the need to pay for adequate coaching, the lack of training facilities, and the usually meager monetary return for swimming compared to other professional sports.

A higher proportion of the "quick-twitch," or white type, muscle fibers has been reported in the muscles of Blacks. The quick-twitch fibers are the ones which contract rapidly and tire easily, as opposed to the slower, but longer-lasting red fibers. What effect the higher ratio of white/red fibers has on muscle density has not been studied. Most of the current research in the components of body mass involves looking at the way fat is proportioned on the body. Fat distribution seems to bear some relationship to constitutional diseases such as diabetes and heart disorders. Studies are in progress to determine racial differences in fat distribution.

Pelvic Size and Related Body Form. Wide shoulders and the V-shaped upper body so prized by body builders is more prevalent in Blacks than in Whites. In reality, there is little or no difference between Blacks and

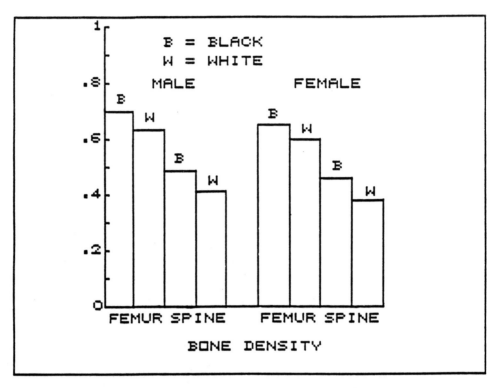

Figure 22. Bone Density in Black and White Males and Females.

Bone density is its weight per unit of volume. Here, volume was calculated by the displacement of millet seed. In bone, hardness can be related to density because they both result from mineralization. Bone densities shown above are based on tests of the femur and vertebrae. The density of the body's various bones are highly correlated, so the femur and spine bones are representative of the entire skeleton. The bar graph above shows that the bones of Blacks are more dense than those of Whites, dependent upon sex. They are also harder. The more dense and hard Black skull is often evident from the color and texture of the bone. These qualities are difficult to quantify, and long experience is required to see a racial difference in these two factors.

Whites in shoulder breadth. Rather, it is the considerably narrower pelvis in Blacks which accounts for the shoulders appearing broader. Figure 23 shows the average pelvic width for Black and White females. The ratio of pelvic width to shoulder width is lower in Blacks in both sexes. White males and Black females are nearly alike with respect to this ratio. The greatest difference occurs between the very low ratio in Black males, indicating a narrow pelvis and comparatively wide shoulders, and the very high ratio in White females, in which the pelvic width can exceed the shoulder width.

Exactly why Blacks and Whites differ in pelvic width is unknown, but

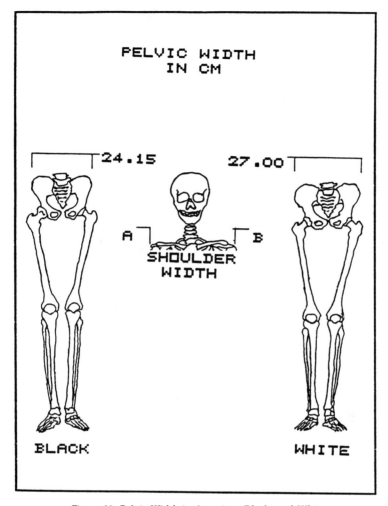

Figure 23. Pelvic Width in American Blacks and Whites.

there is no shortage of possible explanations. The smaller birthweight of the Black baby simply may eliminate the requirement for a wide pelvis. If this is true, the Black pelvis is narrower because nature allows it to be. However, the width of the bony pelvis and the diameter of the outlet required during childbirth may not be closely related. Certainly, racial differences in outlet diameters either have not been studied or the results are not readily available. Another suggestion which has been forwarded is that the White pelvis is a wide base for the proper fitting of a broad torso, and the Black pelvis is a pedestal for the support of a narrow torso. If this suggestion is true, the ultimate source of racial difference would appear to be related to the heat-retention or heat-dissipation function associated with the torso. Still another possibility is that the pelvis is intimately tied up with adaptive differences in locomotion. If an animal walks on two legs, the narrow pelvis contributes to a faster gait. Blacks, with a narrower pelvis, longer lower limbs, and smaller torso to carry, should be able to run faster than Whites. The smaller fuel reserve in the torso should limit the range. Yet, what adaptive significance these features would have in helping Blacks survive is not at all clear unless one accepts the predator theory previously mentioned. To date, the climatic explanation remains the most plausible.

Soft Tissue Features. The more palpable racial features of Blacks have been mentioned only in passing, because virtually everybody is acquainted with them.

The lips of Blacks tend to be thick, but there is not nearly as much difference between Blacks and Whites as there might seem. Lips of Blacks tend to be everted, especially in the female, so that not only is the entire lip visible but a portion of the soft mouth tissue as well. In Whites, the lips are often inverted, or tucked under, so that little or no lip tissue shows on the surface. This is especially the case in the upper lips of many Whites, as can be seen in glamorous notables such as movie stars Kate Jackson and Sam Elliott. Usually, the lip is still present, and plastic surgery can assist in everting it if the individual desires.

The hair follicles on the heads of Blacks are flat, so the hair tends to roll up into tight kinks. This feature sometimes extends to facial and chest hair in the male. The condition can be problematic in a culture where shaving the face is common, because the severed hair shaft turns back and the sharpened end pierces the skin. The coverage, texture and length of underarm and pubic hair is about the same in Blacks and Whites, but the color is more variable in Whites. The pubic hair is typically distributed in a diamond-shaped pattern in the males of both races and in a triangular pattern in the females.

The flaccid penis of the Black male reportedly is comparatively large. The penis of the White male in many cases tends to empty out more blood and shrivel to a greater degree when it is in the unexcited state. The White condition is more concordant with other species of mammals wherein the penis retreats into a sheath and is hardly visible when it is not in use. Probably everyone has noticed the same phenomenon in livestock, especially the horse. There is no discernible difference among the races in the average length or circumference of the erect penis, but individual variability in size and shape is as great as it is in other body structures.

There is a great deal of overlap in skin color between Caucasians and Negroes but virtually none between West Europeans and natives of western Subsaharan Africa. In the United States, the overlap can be so great that affiliation with the Black or White group is often a matter of personal choice. Several dramas have been written concerning this conflict, a situation which has become progressively less dramatic as it has become more common. Still, admixture of the races is far from complete, a subject which is discussed in the last chapter.

5

INTELLIGENCE AND ATHLETICS

Are Whites More Intelligent Than Blacks? Many readers may be too young to remember the 1950s, when intelligence had largely displaced nobility and wealth as a status symbol. It is difficult to exaggerate the value put on intellect in those days, at least in the White community. Suddenly it had become necessary to have a wide range of knowledge. Naturally, the requirement for such intellectual volume would accumulate only in individuals having the highest intelligence test scores. A mother looked upon her child's IQ as the basic measure of his or her worth. Incredible sums of money for the times and prizes galore were bestowed on winners of game shows which purportedly tested the range of an individual's knowledge. Publishers of reference books stressed the woefulness of being "average," a condition which could be remedied by purchasing their line of publications. Politicians either were or were not "eggheads," a term which could be either derisive or respectful, depending on the context, but always referring to the possession of a superior intellect. The "well-rounded man" became the buzz-phrase to describe the product of an ideal education.

In more recent times, intelligence has fairly well lost its celebrity status. Health, physical fitness, and escaping the vagaries of old age have displaced knowledge as the ideal public pursuit. It also has become obvious that mental capacity is not simply a bucket which varies in size among individuals. Learning ability is now known to be complex, with many specific physical factors affecting it other than visual acuity and hearing ability. More than a few intelligent students who were formerly written off as hopeless ignoramuses now would be diagnosed and treated for specific learning disorders. Even more important, as more is learned about intelligence, the more difficult the concept has become to pin down. Some individuals who are mentally non-functional for all practical purposes can perform remarkable feats of the intellect, such as correctly totaling a column of five-digit numbers in their heads or identifying the specific day of the week for June 1, 2049. Such feats could be merely a matter of purposive maximal development of the few faculties remaining in such individuals, but the capability is not fully understood. Even if intelligence is defined arbitrarily as the score on a certain test, variability in intelligence is not accurately reflected by differences in test scores. Psychological statisticians are in fair agreement that there is no meaningful yardstick that can measure the exact distances among test scores. For example, on a standard intelligence test the difference between a score of sixty and ninety is greater than the difference between ninety and one hundred twenty when the subjects' practical performance levels are observed.

For anthropological purposes, the study of identical twins has provided the most useful information about intelligence. Identical twins are genetically the same person. If intelligence is inherent in the physical makeup of individuals, identical twins should make close to the same score on intelligence tests. As it turns out, identical twins do score more alike than do either ordinary brothers and sisters or complementary twins. As it also turns out, identical twins raised together score more alike than do those who are reared in different households. The average difference between the two groups of identical twins—those raised together versus those raised apart—is between ten and fifteen points. This must mean that intelligence is mostly generated by genetic heritage, but environmental effects can exert an average difference of about twelve points.

In the United States, American Whites score an average of at least fifteen points higher than American Blacks on standard intelligence tests. Since a difference in environment is not enough to account for a fifteen-point difference between the races, it has been argued that the native intelligence passed down by the genes is somewhat higher in Whites than it is in Blacks. However, there is considerable evidence that environmental effects have been understated. In a random sample, the probability of selecting middle-class Whites is higher than the chance of selecting individuals from other social strata. Some investigators claim that within each social class, middle-class Whites are brought up under conditions more similar than in any other stratum. If this is true, the overall difference in intelligence scores attributed by environmental effects has been proportionately undervalued. Adoption agencies tend to select adoptive parents who are more similar in social status and income level than would be the case if their names were drawn out of a hat. Foster parent programs and adoption procedures tend to minimize environmental differences between identical twins and other siblings reared apart, because they are placed in similar domiciles.

The most insurmountable obstacle affecting the validity of intelligence tests when more than one race is involved is cultural effect. It is virtually impossible to construct an intelligence test that does not favor the language and values of a particular culture. Tests which emphasize Black vernacular and social values have been put together, and on these tests Whites score significantly lower than Blacks.

Thus, the problems involved in determining a racial difference in intelligence have not been overcome to date. Pure intelligence has proven to be undefinable. Intellect cannot be measured in concrete terms as can most physical traits. If it is defined arbitrarily by test scores, the distances between scores are not uniform. The content, structure, and format of a test are closely related to the cultural values of the people who prepare it. Both genetic and environmental components are involved in testing, and no definitive line can be drawn between their effects. In the light of these problems, speculation on racial differences in intelligence fairly well has been reduced to a prejudicial issue. Anyway, there is so much overlap between Blacks and Whites in test scores that even if a slight difference in averages could be proven, it would be of little practical use.

Are Blacks Better Athletes than Whites? As American Blacks become increasingly dominant in the more popular American sports, so arises the possibility that Blacks might be better athletes by reason of superior physical features. Some of the racial traits which have been presented do seem to meld well with some American sports. Blacks participate in the shorter Olympic track events and in professional basketball in numbers far out of proportion to their representation in the American population. This is commensurate with the racial differences in physical features shown earlier. People with long limbs and small torsos seem to be ready-made for these activities. The construction of larger baseball stadiums has been accompanied by an increase in the number of Black outfielders. Rapid acceleration and high speed for short distances are concordant with Black leg lengths, body proportions, and a greater percentage of quick-twitch muscle fibers. The same features meet a baseball team's requirement to cover the outfield of a large stadium. Not many Blacks are superb competitive swimmers, a fact which goes along with a racial tendency to have poor buoyancy. The arms of Blacks are longer and their skulls are more dense, features which should impart superiority in boxing, and sure enough more Blacks than Whites fight for a living.

There can be no doubt that individual Blacks have excelled in sports, and such excellence can be quantified in terms of medals and money. However, to claim that racial characters are the sole, or even the major, reason for the success of Blacks in American athletics probably is not very accurate. Unique personal achievement in sports has been evident in individuals of many races and ethnic groups; it speaks more for individual variation in physique, talent and resolution than it does for an advantage due to racial traits. Similarly, the successes of racially or ethnically segregated teams are not consistent enough to establish any effect of race. In the 1920s and 1930s, one of the earliest Black basketball teams, the Renaissance Big Five, beat the all-White Boston Celtics more or less whenever they wanted to, and regarded themselves as world champions. But so did the South Philadelphia Hebrew Association. On the other side of the coin, the all-White Soviets clearly bested the virtually all-Black United States basketball team in the 1988 Olympic Games. Neither individual achievement nor segregated teams make much of a statement about the effect of race. In fact, national affiliation seems to be more influential. A single country may dominate a particular event for years, as evidenced by the weight lifters of Bulgaria and the high jumpers of East Germany. National emphasis, funding, and coaching are no doubt highly responsible for such success stories.

From an anthropological viewpoint, there are two good reasons why racial characters alone cannot account for the success of Blacks in American sports. One, considering the overlap in physical features of Blacks and Whites, and the proportions of Blacks and Whites in the American population, the racial features which might be useful in a certain sport can be found in a great number of both Blacks and Whites. The fact that many Blacks eventually emerge from this pool as contenders for professional positions must have more to do with behavior and the social setting rather than racial traits. Two, the distribution of Blacks among sports which can exploit Black racial traits indicates a purposive rather than a random arrangement of those traits. For example, the physical features of Blacks are well-suited to the needs of both volleyball and basketball. Yet, the American volleyball team sent to the twenty-fourth Olympic Games in 1988 had not a single Black on the team. The basketball team was virtually all Black. Factors other than physical features must be at work to account for the visibility of Blacks in boxing and on professional basketball, football, and baseball teams.

In the recent past, playing a professional sport, along with music and dance, were the few major ways that American Blacks could be successful. Racial barriers collapse on the bandstand, in the ring, and on the court or field. It is likely that maximum development of athletic talent has been, and is, stressed and rewarded, however unconsciously or indirectly, by the Black family and community. It also seems likely that there is a systematic exclusion of those sports which do not earn big money. It would be my guess that a sandlot volleyball game would be laughed out of a Black intercity neighborhood.

The scarcity of conflicting opportunities may play a significant role in the emotional stability and mental resolution which guide Blacks to sports success. Historically, American Blacks have not been required to suffer much agony over whether to pursue an uncertain career in sports, or to take over Dad's dealership and marry Billie Jo. An intense personal motivation, the lack of a comparable opportunity elsewhere, the acclaim of family and community, and the possibility of wealth and fame are probably the factors more responsible for the visibility of Black athletes in specific sports than any biological advantage. A parallel can be drawn with regard to the participation of Blacks in the social sciences. Archaeology, physical anthropology, cultural anthropology, sociology, and social work are all social sciences. Virtually no Black involvement exists in the first three fields, but sociology and especially social work draw many Blacks. The work in sociology and social work is aimed at solutions to problems that Blacks have confronted in the past and which they face to a somewhat lesser extent today.

There is at least some evidence that the success of Blacks in American sports has as much to do with showmanship as anything else. In basketball particularly, the advent of Blacks on American teams seems to have had more to do with changing the style of play rather than adding significantly to the scoreboard. Figure 24 shows the average season basketball scores for White teams at three southern universities. Each team made some progress, on the average, in scoring more points per season for the sixteen seasons between 1956 and 1971. This is evident by the gradual upslope of the lines approximating the average season scores. The popular notion is that the addition of Blacks to the teams has increased the upslope, and more points are being scored than ever before. Yet, as is evident in Figure 25, the average season scores of the same three basketball teams has significantly decreased in the sixteen years since Blacks have come to dominate the game. The teams shown are by no means a valid random sample, but they were selected by me on the basis of exigency rather than expectation. There is no a priori reason why the examination of similar teams should not produce similar results.

The nature of American basketball also has changed since integration. For a view of the old style of playing, one must go to Europe where it is still in vogue. The European game has a sort of stiff, earthbound quality when compared to the more fluid, airborne game played here. The newer approach makes American basketball a basically faster, more graceful and inventive game to watch.

There can be no doubt that some American sports, especially basket-

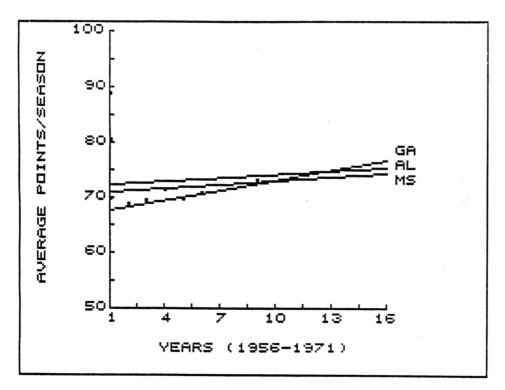

Figure 24. Average Season Basketball Scores for 1956 to 1971 at the Universities of Alabama, Georgia, and Mississippi.

Each line represents the pathway which comes the closest to all of the average scores for each of the three university teams. All three teams gradually improved in the total number of points scored for the sixteen year period 1956 through 1971. The team members during this time span were White.

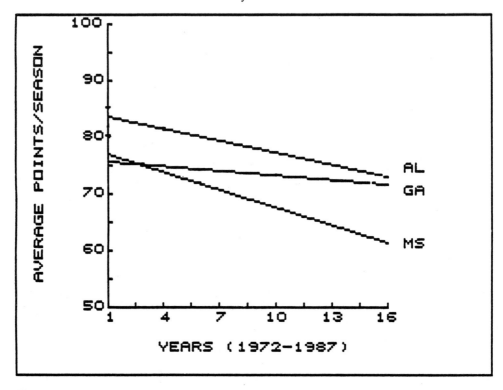

Figure 25. Average Season Basketball Scores for 1972 to 1987 at the Universities of Alabama, Georgia, and Mississippi.

Each line represents the pathway which comes the closest to all of the average scores for each of the three university teams. All three teams gradually worsened in the total number of points scored for the sixteen year period 1972 through 1987. Each team became increasingly dominated by Black players during this time span. Exactly what this means is unclear, because the same players conduct both defense and offense, but there can be no doubt that the average number of successful goals has decreased since the teams became racially integrated.

ball and football, have become increasingly marked by events of individual showmanship. How and when talent and showmanship became melded is nebulous, but the two qualities are now closely integrated. The initial inroads of Blacks into American athletics were laid by no-nonsense sports figures having pure measurable talent. Jesse Owens broke speed and distance records, Joe Louis put numbers of opponents on the canvas, and Jackie Robinson added runs to his side of the scoreboard and kept them off the other side. But show business had been the path to Black success long before integration. Even in sports alone, Black teams such as the Harlem Globe-Trotters were enjoyed mostly for their clowning and semi-serious ball handling, albeit superior, rather than baskets scored. During the watershed years of the early 1970s, the influx of Black athletes into White schools exerted pressure on the coaches to align their tactics more concordantly with the traditional show-business Black style of play. White coaches who before would have chastised a player severely for "fancy stuff" suddenly began to allow more freedom of athletic expression. The rigid military drill historically inflicted on White athletes became especially relaxed for Black players, perhaps through the coaches' collective fear of reprisal by organized Blacks carrying legal and political clout. As the young athletes advanced into professional American sports, basketball and football in particular came to be imbued with a Black brand of showmanship. In turn, new crops of young athletes emulated the professionals, promoting the growth of a jubilant style of play which formerly would not have been tolerated on all-White teams.

The fans loved it.

It is interesting to ponder what different scoring rules now might be in effect had basketball been invented and promoted by Blacks to start with. As it is, the appreciation of athletic creativity and showmanship can only be quantified in terms of attendance instead of points. A tomahawk or a slam dunk might as well be a conventional layup, and a skyhook could be a set shot as far as the scoreboard is concerned.

In summary, there seems to be no convincing evidence that Whites are smarter than Blacks or that Blacks enjoy any racial advantage in sports. The dearth of Black talent in the more cerebral endeavors can be laid to the effects of segregation. Why learn to be a stockbroker if there is little hope of finding a job? Besides, that situation is changing. Blacks are beginning to find employment in engineering, banking, computer science, and so forth, and a Black middle class now is burgeoning in major American metropolitan areas. It seems likely that once the socioeconomic condition of Blacks is truly on a par with that of Whites, a more proportionate distribution of Blacks among all of the professions, including sports—big money-making or not—will follow.

6

RACIAL FEATURES AND ADAPTATION

Introduction. All animal species, including humans, biologically adapt to the environment. Humans, equipped with a protective technology, are not required to adapt as fast as animals. Technology not only acts as a dampener to biological change within each human group but also assists gene flow among groups by improving transportation. This human advantage provided by technology is obvious from the fact that people from all over the world remain capable of reproducing with each other in spite of thousands of years of adapting to different environments.

The adaptive model proposed in this chapter is based upon the exploitation of energy resources. It explains racial differences in early development—but not adult racial features—in terms of the relative abundance of energy in Africa, Europe, and North America.

Assumptions of the Model. Africa is considered to be the source of the world's human beings. Attempts to prove this have been convincing to anthropologists, but by no means does everybody accept it. From archaeological evidence, it is certain that people have occupied Africa longer than any other continent. Human-like beings, both hominids and hominoids, lived there for an inconceivable length of time before modern people came on the scene. Races as we know them developed long after the diaspora of humans, presumably from Africa to Asia and Europe, thence to other continents.

Since all species reproduce fairly rapidly up to the point of crowding, the African continent must have been overpopulated for thousands upon thousands of years. It remains crowded today. In response, the inhabitants must have developed survival strategies somewhat different from those developed by people who were not so constrained by the need for resources. The development of a biological survival strategy is not, of course, a purposive undertaking. Rather, it is a biological process which has operated in favor of a people's survival through time.

Archaeological evidence indicates that for most of Subsaharan Africa's history, its people existed at the small group level of social organization, probably no larger than the tribe. Intense competition was likely the rule among individuals of a tribe, and warfare must have been frequent among the various tribes. To be sure, organization at the city-state and kingdom levels was not unknown in Africa, but this happened fairly recently from a biological perspective of time. Important is the fact that for most of its history Subsaharan Africa was occupied mainly by pockets of people, the vast majority of whom never enjoyed a long-term surplus of resources. In this situation, adults are the most important members of the group. Under crowded conditions, adults are the means by which the group gathers energy-producing resources, because the young cannot compete effectively. The success or failure of adults dictates whether or not the group will survive through time. The energy required to produce new adults therefore has real impact on the pool of available energy which is not overflowing to begin with.

If Africans have been crowded for most of their existence, American Indians have been at the other extreme. Occupation of North and South America came late, and resources abounded. Energy was not a precious commodity. The aboriginal population was probably still expanding when Columbus arrived. In this environment, threats to survival are unpredictable, the adult is not so important, and competition for resources is low. Each individual stands about as good a chance of surviving as another. Under these conditions, one survival strategy is to produce as many offspring as possible. The adult is fairly expendable, and new individuals need not be particularly free of defects to survive. Resources are bountiful and energy can be wasted.

Europe falls between Africa and the Americas as far as the length of time the land has been occupied. However, successive increases in food production on a large scale apparently have been the rule in Europe for thousands of years. Previously, anthropologists thought that only the idea of farming spread rapidly throughout Europe, and the various tribes took up farming and the settled life at about the same time. Now there is fairly good evidence that farmers themselves spread from the Near East across Europe, both displacing the original tribal-oriented inhabitants and incorporating the tribes into the food-producing community. This was not a purposive march from east to west but an expansion in that direction as populated areas filled with people. Meanwhile, food production must have become increasingly more efficient, with new ideas spreading among the farmers, permitting population expansion in already cultivated areas. Under these conditions, biological responses resulting in racial features would be more complex, but the expectation is that the racial characters imparted by such responses would be somewhere between the African and American Indian extremes.

It is important to realize that the extremes of environmental differences have been emphasized. On a yearly basis, Africa could not have been all famine, nor the New World all feast. The more reasonable assumption is that there were periods of want and plenty no matter what the geographic area. But Africans, because of crowded conditions, must have had a tendency to adapt more toward the famine side of existence, while American Indians must have adapted more toward the feast side. Europeans should fall somewhere between the extremes. The proposal here is that over thousands of generations, some adaptive features have accrued in response to these different average leanings, however variable they might have been during the short time periods marked by either want or plenty.

The Adaptive Model. If the conditions outlined above have actually taken place—and there is no reason to suspect that they did not—the racial differences in early development among Blacks, Whites, and native Americans can be explained. One would expect that American Indians alive today would be marked by rapid fetal development, the largest birthweights, and the highest incidence of birth defects. These features would be the logical outcome of thousands of years of producing large numbers of offspring in an environment rich with resources. Blacks, subject to a more intensive biological control, should develop the slowest, be the smallest at birth, and be the most free of developmental errors. These characters would reflect long-term penny-pinching with respect to the available energy in a crowded environment. Whites should be somewhere between the two.

Tests of the Model. The adaptive model melds well with the information which has already been presented for Blacks in the early stages of development and in infancy. Black babies are smaller than Whites at birth, the incidence of developmental error is lower, and development of Blacks seems to be slower for nearly three years after conception. The developmental errors for which data is available on all three races also seem to be distributed in favor of the model. In fact, the racial differences in the incidences of some developmental errors can be staggering. As shown by Figure 26, cleft uvula is nearly forty times more frequent in American Indians than in Blacks, and over ten times higher than the incidence in Whites. The uvula is the triangular-shaped structure in the back of the throat. Although a cleft in the uvula has never been a threat to survival, it does represent some slop in the developmental process. Had the process been just a bit more sloppy, cleft palate probably would have been the result. It is important to remember that conceiving, developing, birthing, and rearing offspring takes a tremendous amount of energy. If the offspring is seriously defective, the energy has been wasted. Among American Indians, this would have made little difference. Among Blacks, the possibility of cleft palate, and the subsequent waste of precious energy when the defective individual died, would have had more impact on group survival. Thus, it is highly probable that developmental error of the magnitude found in American Indians would not have been tolerated in the Black developmental system.

The adaptive model also fits neatly with the observed birthweights of the three races. The average birthweight of Blacks is six pounds, Whites average seven pounds, and the American Indian newborn averages seven and one-quarter pounds. The average Black birthweight distinctly stands out from the other two, there being four times as much difference between Blacks and Whites than the difference between Whites and American Indians.

Another anomaly which dramatizes the disparity in birth defects among the races involves the backbone. The vertebrae which enclose the spinal cord develop from several bones which normally fuse to form a complete protective ring around the cord. Failure of the bones to meet and fuse leaves a gap called neural arch defect or separate neural arch. It usually occurs in the lower back. The racial differences in this error are graphically portrayed in Figure 27. The error is over ten times more common in American Indians than in Blacks, and over twice as frequent in Whites as it is in the Blacks. Like cleft uvula, neural arch defect poses no threat to survival, and it apparently has no impact on physical ability. It simply represents a degradation in the developmental trajectory.

Cleft lip/palate and cleft uvula are assumed to be related disorders, with cleft uvula being much the less intense manifestation of the same basic error in development. The palate forms from two plates which grow toward the midline and eventually meet in the middle. The tongue is in the way when the plates begin to grow, but it normally drops down in plenty of time to let the plates pass overhead and fuse. If the tongue is late, the result can be cleft uvula, cleft palate, or cleft lip and palate, depending on how late the tongue is. The tongue in turn depends upon the timely completion of other structures before it can drop down, so the timing and control process is integrated and highly complex.

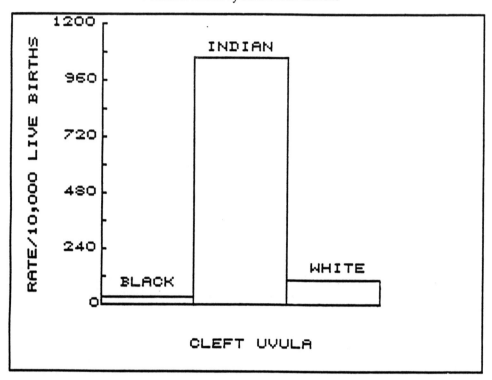

Figure 26. Incidence of Cleft Uvula in Blacks, American Indians, and Whites.

The uvula is the triangular-shaped structure which dangles from the back of the soft palate. A cleft in the uvula is a rather minor birth defect and is completely survivable. However, it probably indicates a near miss for cleft palate, a more serious developmental error in which the bony plates which form the roof of the mouth fail to meet in the centerline. American Indians exhibit an unusually high frequency of cleft uvula. In American Blacks, the condition is quite rare by comparison. Whites are in between, but much closer to Blacks. This distribution is concordant with expectations of the adaptive model proposed in the text.

The incidences of cleft lip/palate and congenital heart defect are shown in Figures 28 and 29, respectively. Cleft lip/palate is distributed among the three races virtually exactly in accordance with the expectations of the proposed adaptive model. The incidence of congenital heart defect is higher in Blacks than would be expected, but still it is the lowest among the three races.

The frequencies of spina bifida, anencephalus, and clubfoot are not exactly concordant with the adaptive model, particularly with respect to Whites. Spina bifida is a condition in which the muscle, connective tissue, and skin fail to come together over the spinal cord, leaving it open to the environment. The defect frequently is not survivable today and

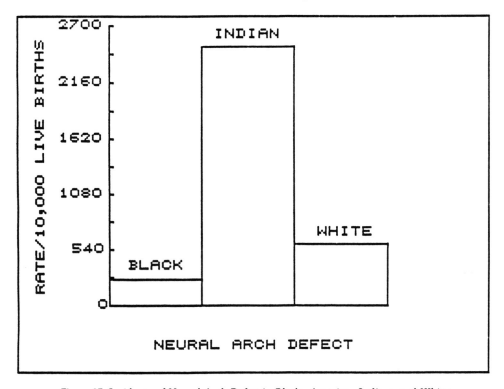

Figure 27. Incidence of Neural Arch Defect in Blacks, American Indians, and Whites.

The neural arch is the back part of the bony ring on each vertebra containing the vertebral spine. The vertebral spines are the elevations visible beneath the skin in the chest portion of the backbone. If the neural arch does not fuse with the rest of the vertebra, the condition is known as neural arch defect. The defect is the most common among American Indians, as is evident in the above bar graph. The distribution argues in favor of the adaptive model. Blacks are the lowest and Whites are intermediate in the distribution of the defect among the three races. The condition is not disabling and has no apparent impact on survivability.

was likely never survived aboriginally. For some reason, American Indians appear to be protected from defects such as anencephalus and spina bifida, both of which occur early in the development process. About seven American Indians are affected by spina bifida for every five Blacks and thirteen Whites. The incidence of anencephalus is even slightly lower in American Indians than in Blacks; the difference between the two races is not statistically significant, but it is a distinct departure from ideal expectations of the adaptive model. Clubfoot frequencies are the same in Blacks as in American Indians. Here again, the incidence in Whites is higher than would be expected. Figures 30 through 32 graphically present these three birth defects.

In spite of the frequencies demonstrated for the last three defects,

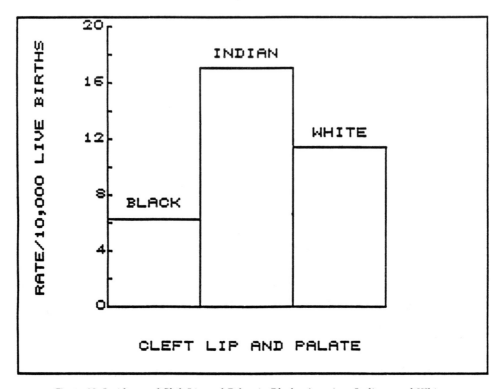

Figure 28. Incidence of Cleft Lip and Palate in Blacks, American Indians, and Whites.

When the two bony plates in the roof of the mouth, and all of the soft tissue structures associated with these plates fail to meet in the midline, the condition is called cleft lip and palate. The severity varies according to the width of the cleft, most cases being correctable today with surgery. In aboriginal times, it is unlikely that any form of this defect could have been survived on a regular basis. The distribution of the developmental error among the three races meets the expectations of the proposed adaptive model quite well, with Blacks being the lowest, American Indians the highest, and Whites intermediate in frequency.

overall, the information on developmental errors of all three races tends to support the adaptive model. Of the seven developmental errors presented, American Indians have the highest frequency in four, and Whites are highest in three. Blacks are never the highest. In fact, Blacks are the lowest in five of the seven birth defects, equal to the lowest in one, and not significantly higher than the lowest in the last one. Blacks fit the model very well.

This is usually as good as biological information ever gets in support of a general model, especially if the model has to do with human beings. While there can be no doubt that humans adapt biologically, the process is complex at the outset, and cultural practices interfere and further complicate it. Besides, progress in technology—tools, fire, and food

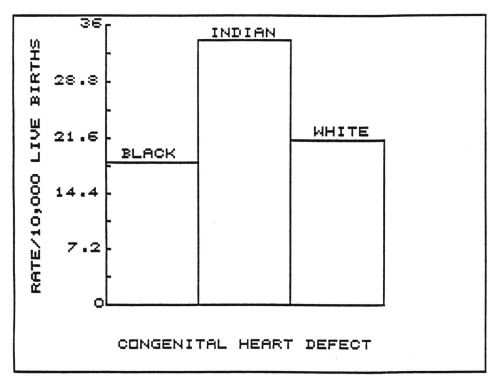

Figure 29. Incidence of Congenital Heart Defect in Blacks, American Indians, and Whites.

Congenital heart defects are developmental errors of the heart. Manifestations vary from relatively minor defects to the near absence of major structures. Presently, there is no way of determining which forms would or would not have been survivable under aboriginal conditions. It is probable that the competitive effectiveness of individuals who suffered from the condition would have been reduced, especially in environments where resources were scarce. The distribution of the defect fits the expectations of the adaptive model fairly well. American Indians suffer the condition most frequently, Blacks the least, and Whites are in between.

production, for example—is the much greater component working toward the survival of human groups. As was earlier mentioned, in spite of thousands of years of isolation and dissimilation, human beings remain interfertile regardless of the racial features which have come to imbue each geographic group. Presumably, technology alone has permitted this to be true.

The proposed model seems able to explain adequately the features of early development in Blacks. Slow development permits a more error-free development and a smaller birthweight. In turn, a small birthweight helps to protect the mother. All of these features are related to energy conservation. They are of utmost biological importance in a crowded environment where resources are scarce.

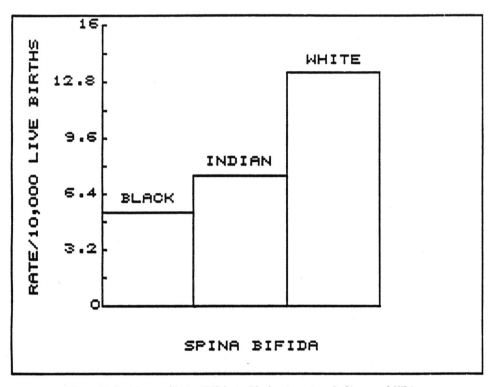

Figure 30. Incidence of Spina Bifida in Blacks, American Indians, and Whites.

In spina bifida, the baby is born with the spinal cord open to the elements. It is a major birth defect involving elements of the back which normally fuse to form a protective covering for the cord. The condition is often not survivable even today. There is little doubt that any manifestation of the developmental error would have been mortal outside of modern times. In this defect, Blacks, Indians and Whites do not exactly fit the adaptive model because of the relatively high frequency in Whites. Still, Blacks demonstrate the lowest incidence of the defect. It is not likely that this error is related to neural arch defect in any way except location.

Adaptation and Features of Youth and Adulthood. The adaptive processes responsible for racial features in early human development are easily explainable compared to the processes responsible for adult traits. The successful production of a new individual is almost wholly confined to biological properties as far as the offspring's survival is concerned. These biological properties are responsible for some Black traits well beyond the early development phase. The higher degree of right-left symmetry in Blacks, and the relatively high numbers of Blacks who develop normal third molars, are two adult features which can be attributed to a more intense control of the early developmental system.

But normally in adulthood, other complicating factors come into play. Adult features are under the influence of a more interactive system in

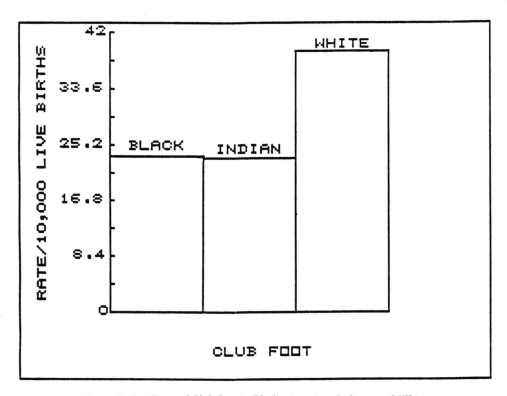

Figure 31. Incidence of Club Foot in Blacks, American Indians, and Whites.

Club foot is somewhat exceptional to the expectations of the adaptive model. American Indians have a low incidence of this birth disorder compared to other malformations, as low as American Blacks. Whites suffer the defect in numbers almost twice as high as the other two races. The racial distribution of the defect in Blacks and Whites fit the model quite well, but the frequency in American Indians cannot be explained except as possible underreporting of the disorder.

which technology, behavior, and other cultural elements interfere with biological components of change. Such factors serve to complicate the adaptive process and make it difficult if not impossible to interpret. Who will reproduce and pass on their genes, and in what numbers of new individuals, depends not only on biological fitness but also on social structure and cultural values. In societies which have been observed, the number of adults who actually produce offspring is consistently less than the number who are biologically capable of doing so. Opportunity, social role, voluntary celibacy, sexual disinterest, homosexuality and other behavioral components affect the production of new individuals. The physical features of adults also can be propagated because of their perceived aesthetic qualities or other virtues of cultural value rather

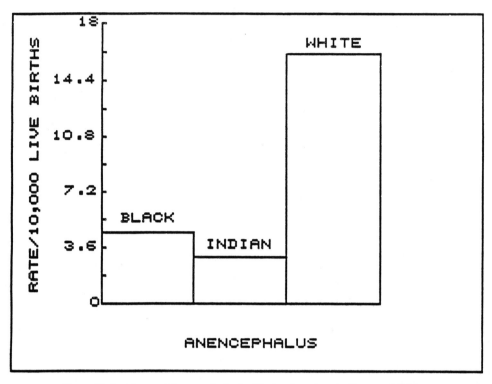

Figure 32. Incidence of Anencephalus in Blacks, American Indians, and Whites.

This defect is the failure of the brain to develop. It is probable that both spina bifida and anencephalus are developmental errors which occur early in the developmental phase. For some reason, American Indians appear to be protected from early disorders in development. The frequencies of anencephalus in Whites and American Indians do not meet the expectations of the adaptive model. Whites exhibit a very high incidence of the defect; Blacks have a slightly, but not significantly higher frequency than American Indians. The distribution of biological information often fails to follow the rule, so this exception is not greatly surprising.

than their biological utility. Milky white skin is highly valued in Japan, for example. The reverse can also be true; it has been shown that redheaded men and women couple with each other in fewer numbers than would be expected by chance alone. For some reason there is a modicum of mutual avoidance among people having red hair.

Some adult human traits, such as body shape and limb lengths, are explainable because they are aligned with similar traits in animals dwelling in the same geographic area. Presumably, such features have been produced by the same or similar processes in both humans and animals. The possible effect of climate on limb lengths and proportions was mentioned when these features were presented earlier. Other adult traits can still be attributed to environmental effects, but because of cultural interactions, the features are uniquely human. The sheer body size of both Blacks and Whites is puzzling from a purely biological perspective. People about the size of a gymnast—roughly five feet in height, one hundred thirty pounds—enjoy the highest strength/weight ratios and still remain well within the boundaries of normal human variability. There is no good biological reason to be any bigger. The nose is another adult feature which does not follow biological expectations if animals are used for comparison. High-latitude mammals nearly all have short, stubby snouts, while humans have long, thin, projecting noses. In low latitudes, the reverse is the case in both humans and animals. Humans, of course, operate in arctic climates assisted by fire and clothing, and cultural factors such as these must direct the biological responses in a way that is peculiar to the human species.

The difficulty in accounting for the impact of cultural factors is that many such factors may be evanescent from the perspective of biological change through time. It has been well-established that in American society today, male stature is rewarded socially and economically. But how long this value has persisted in the past is unknown. Nor has the effect of stature on fecundity been extensively studied even in modern groups. Historically, human groups which have migrated to a different area are composed of individuals who are taller on the average than those who have remained in place. Again, how long this has been true is unknown. It seems possible that a trait such as body size also could have more to do with the behavior of humans toward each other than with environmental interactions. In low-technology cultures, warfare among groups and physical competition among individuals favor the production of larger and stronger people. In any case, the adaptive processes which have produced and perpetuated many adult traits must have been very complex, now obscuring the reason why such features are in existence. The Australian Aborigine and the African native of the Kalahari Desert are about as far apart in anatomy as two people can get. Yet, the climate and technologies of each are as close as they can come and still be different.

In short, why and how traits such as hair type, lip size and shape, skull features, and the like came to be what they are is anybody's guess. As more is learned, it should become possible to formulate a testable model which includes adult features, despite the indecipherment of many of them today.

7

CONCLUDING REMARKS ON
BLACK RACIAL FEATURES

Overview of Racial Traits. The stereotyped American Black can be defined by the traits which have been presented herein. He or she develops slowly and accurately and is well protected from toxins introduced into the mother. The birthweight is small, right and left body parts are symmetrical, and the chances of a birth defect are low. These racial traits have accrued in response to an environment in which resources are precious. As the infant grows, development lags for a couple of years and then accelerates. Teeth begin to erupt earlier than they do in Whites, and the Black child becomes a bit taller. In adulthood, the body is denser, the torso shorter, the pelvis narrower, and the limbs are longer. Arm and leg segments are more equal in length than in Whites. The skull is fairly smooth, the forehead vertical, and the brow ridges reduced or absent. The eyes are separated by a wide wedge of bone, and both eyes frequently are visible when the head is near the profile position. The eye sockets are squarish, the nasal opening short and wide. The front teeth are large, and the muzzle projects forward.

By contrast, the adult White has limbs which are shortened, more so in the distal segments. The torso is long and the pelvis is wide. The skull is rugged, with receding forehead and robust brow ridges. The upper face and nose projects forward so that one eye usually is well-hidden when the head is turned toward the side. The eye sockets are roundish. The nose is long and narrow. The front teeth are small, and the muzzle is flat.

Some people believe that Blacks originated by the breeding of Whites with African apes. Many people still maintain that this silly story is biblically based. Aside from the fact that such couplings cannot produce an offspring, it is interesting to note that in most of the racial features which have been presented, Blacks are farther from apes than are Whites. The length of the upper arm relative to the forearm is more ape-like in

74

Blacks than in Whites, but a long torso in relation to leg length, a rugged skull with heavy brow ridges, front teeth which are small relative to the molars, and the late development of canine teeth are all traits more apish in Whites than in Blacks. Such comparisons are not much more than exercises in interesting trivia, because the physical differences among human races are virtually nil compared to the biological differences between humans and apes.

The stereotyped American Black (or White) usually is not the real thing. In the flesh, the traits vary. I have tried to emphasize the degree of overlap among the races in any particular physical feature and the fact that racial definitions are dependent upon differences in averages. Still, the observable traits which have been mentioned are all usually visible in a group of Blacks of eight or so people, especially in the rural South, where admixture of the races has not proceeded as far as it has in metropolitan areas.

Among American Blacks and Whites, no concrete evidence supports any marked differences in capabilities and limitations which might be influenced by racial features. Blacks seem to be as intelligent as Whites, and Whites appear to be as athletic as Blacks. The visibility of Whites in fields which require intellectual achievement, and the conspicuousness of Blacks in professions which exploit physical prowess seem to be merely the current upshots of American cultural history. If Whites had been able to tolerate intellect, pride, and dignity in Blacks historically, no racial feature would have prevented Blacks from a representative share of authoritative positions today. Similarly, if Whites had been channeled into the entertainment professions, crowd-pleasing expressions of exhilaration and style probably would be more manifest in Whites, particularly the athletes.

Admixture of American Blacks and Whites. Pure African or European ancestries are mostly mythical in families which for many generations have resided in America. People claiming such a bloodline really mean "almost pure," with "almost" being undefined. Even if such lineages could be traced accurately, White settlers and Black slaves probably shared some genes in common when they first set foot on American soil. The geographic sources of American Blacks and Whites just aren't far enough apart to completely stop the flow of genes. It is much easier for genes to flow between Europe and Africa than, say, between Europe and Australia. Certainly, Caucasians and Negroes are genetically closer to each other than Negroes are to Mongoloids or Mongoloids are to

Caucasians. When blood antigens, enzymes, and blood types are tabulated, Caucasians and Negroes aren't all that far apart.

Americans have a greater degree of Black and White admixture than their ancestors in West Europe and West Africa. Admixture in the United States has been scientifically tested on many occasions, always with the same results: Blacks have a relatively high proportion of West European genes, and Whites have a relatively low proportion of West African genes. These results are not at all surprising in light of the social history of America. They state succinctly that in this country more genes have flowed from White to Black than from Black to White. Still, there has been a definite flow in each direction, so American Blacks and Whites have a genetic structure somewhere between that found in West Europe and West Africa.

One way that the admixture is obvious in American Blacks and Whites is skin color. Although there is a great deal of overlap in skin color between Caucasians and Negroes, there is little or no overlap between West Europeans and West Africans. The overlap here in America is so great that affiliation with the Black or White group is often a matter of some obscurity.

A study which demonstrated a less obvious but equally pervasive admixture was conducted years ago in Claxton, Georgia. The investigators showed that one gene with frequencies of 47 percent in European Whites and zero in African Blacks was at frequencies of 42 percent in Claxton Whites and 5 percent in Claxton Blacks. Another gene at 3 percent in West Europeans and 60 percent in West Africans was found at 4 percent of Claxton Whites and 54 percent of Claxton Blacks. Every gene which was tested was found to be at some frequency "X" in our European ancestors, at "Y" frequency in our African ancestors, and somewhere between "X" and "Y" in the Claxton population. Carrying the same type of study further, genes were found to be most admixed in people from Detroit, then Oakland, followed in decreasing order by upstate New York, Claxton, and Charleston. These results fit in very well with the known social history of these localities. For American Blacks and Whites in general, there is no doubt that the proportion of European and African ancestry is a matter of degree. These findings satisfyingly fit the old anthropological adage about different human groups encountering each other for the first time: battle is possible, but breeding is certain.

Future of the Races. Racial features have been presented as geographically induced phenomena. The significance of geography as an isolating mechanism lies in the past when races were formed. Prejudice, economics, politics, and language are the main barriers to gene flow among the races today. Although English is rapidly becoming universally understood, and the Western media are distributing their wares throughout the world, the effect on racial admixture has not been very apparent. Nevertheless, it must be presumed that as we move toward a world culture, someday racial differences will go out of existence. The time required for that to happen should be quite short from a biological perspective of time, but certainly not a noticeable event in any few generations.

Within the United States, there is no reason that Black and White genes should not continue to flow together. Desegregation of the schools, and the isolation of individuals from family members and peer groups—as occurs in metropolitan areas—should act as accelerants to the commingling process.

EPILOGUE

Looking back over the contents of this book, I believe that most anthropologists would agree with the bulk of what is included here. The concept of slow development in Blacks is the most controversial aspect of this book. The reader will find no problem locating views to the contrary if he or she so desires. In fact, A. P. Polednak in his excellent 1986 review of the subject (see "Bibliography") proposed the opposite idea: Blacks develop fast and thereby tend to get past the danger points early. Paradoxically, our views may not be all that far apart. Development of a human being is highly complex, and it involves careful timing and control of both constructive and destructive processes. A Black developmental scenario might incorporate a lengthy delay until conditions are optimal to proceed on to a rapid constructive or destructive phase. A more relaxed mode of White development might proceed under suboptimal conditions, construct and destroy at a slower pace, yet take less time overall to get the job completed. There is also the possibility of rapid destruction being accompanied by slow construction and vice versa. Considering that even with X-rays, ultrasound, and magnetic resonance imaging, we get only a very few peeks at a very few pregnancies, there is no shortage of places where racial variation might fit into the developmental picture. I favor the idea of slow development in Blacks for a couple of reasons. One, the linear measurements which point to slower development involve teeth, and teeth are a single structure of simple composition and morphology. A measurement such as the biparietal diameter, which Polednak uses as an indicator that Blacks develop rapidly, not only spans the brain, brain coverings, vessels, venous sinuses, bone and skin, but can also can vary because of variability in the geometry of the head. Thus, it is not clear exactly what is being measured, but whatever it is the dimension could have as much to do with shape as it does with size. Another reason I favor a slow development scenario is that factors which tend to verify the linear measurement of teeth, and thereby verify a slow development in Blacks, are independent of linear measurement. Tooth eruption, tooth replacement, and completion of the fingerprints are directly observable developmental events. There is no doubt that Blacks and Whites differ in the onset of these events, with Blacks lagging behind Whites for nearly three years after conception. Also, Polednak's concept of faster development doesn't fit very well with the observation that miscarried Blacks reach stages of fingerprint maturity in advance of normal Black unborns.

Although this book is not directed at professionals in anthropology or human biology, a bibliography is included for readers who would like to read additional material on the subjects discussed herein or who might want to repeat and verify the graphic information contained in the figures. Figures 1, 11, and 12 are direct plots of the means (averages) given in Garn (1985). Figures 2 and 3 connect the means provided by Kraus and Jordan (1965) and Roberts (1969), respectively. Figure 4 shows tabular data included in Garn et al. (1973). Figures 5, 9, and 10 are linear least-squares regressions of the ridge maturity information contained in Babler's (1977) work. Figures 6, 7, and 8 are plots of both Taffel's data and that of Polednak (1986). Figures 13, 14, and 15 are plots for males given by Malina and associates in Martorell et al. (1988). Figures 16 through 23 are descriptive and bone measurement data which can be found in Krogman's (1962) excellent reference which has been recently updated (1986) with the able assistance of M. Y. Iscan. Figures 24 and 25 are least-squares linear regressions on data which can be obtained in any basketball media guide (1987 or later) for the Universities of Alabama, Georgia, and Mississippi. All the scores for each season were first summarized by means, and the season means for each team were regressed on years. Figures 26 through 32 are simply graphic summarizations of the data contained in the following works: Erickson (1976), Heathcote (1974), Niswander et al. (1975), and Roche and Rowe (1951). The remainder of the bibliography represents sources for much, but not all, of the information which was mentioned in the text; it is, of course, impossible to provide a reference for every fact of a descriptive nature that one has learned, verified, and internalized.

BIBLIOGRAPHY

Ammerman, Albert J., and Cavalli-Sforza, Luigi L.: *The Neolithic Transition and the Genetics of Populations in Europe.* Princeton, Princeton University Press, 1984.

Babler, W. J.: The prenatal origins of population differences in human dermatoglyphics. Ph.D. Dissertation, University of Michigan, 1977.

Bass, William M.: *Human Osteology: A Laboratory and Field Manual.* Columbia, Missouri Archaeological Society, 1971.

Brues, Alice M.: *People and Races.* New York, Macmillan, 1977.

Dyer, K. F.: Patterns of gene flow between Negroes and Whites in the United States. *Journal of Biosocial Science, 8:* 309–333, 1976.

Erickson, J. D.: Racial variation in the incidence of congenital malformations. *Annals of Human Genetics, 39:* 315–320, 1976.

Excoffier, L., Pellegrini, B., Sanchez-Mazas, A., Simon, C., and Langaney, A.: Genetics and history of Sub-Saharan Africa. *Yearbook of Physical Anthropology, 30:* 151–194, 1987.

Garn, S. M.: Smoking and human biology. *Human Biology, 57:* 505–523, 1985.

Garn, S. M., Sandusky, S. T., Nagy, J. M., and Trowbridge, F. L.: Negro-Caucasoid differences in permanent tooth emergence at a constant income level. *Archives of Oral Biology, 18:* 609–615, 1973.

Harris, Joseph E.: *Africans and Their History,* 2nd ed. New York, NAL Penguin, 1987.

Heathcote, G. M.: The prevalence of cleft uvula in an Inuit population. *American Journal of Physical Anthropology, 41:* 433–438, 1974.

Iscan, M. Y.: Rise of forensic anthropology. *Yearbook of Physical Anthropology, 31:* 203–230, 1988.

Jantz, R. L.: Population variation in asymmetry and diversity from finger to finger for digital ridge counts. *American Journal of Physical Anthropology, 42:* 215–224, 1975.

Kraus, Bertram S., and Jordan, Ronald E.: *The Human Dentition Before Birth.* Philadelphia, Lea and Febiger, 1965.

Krogman, Wilton M.: *The Human Skeleton in Forensic Medicine.* Springfield, Thomas, 1962.

Malina, R. M., Little, B. B., Shoup, R. F., and Buschang, P. H.: Adaptive significance of small body size: strength and motor performance of school children in Mexico and Papua, New Guinea. *American Journal of Physical Anthropology, 73:* 489–499, 1987.

Martorell, R., Malina, R. M., Castillo, R. O., Mendoza, F. S., and Pawson, I. G.: Body proportions in three ethnic groups: children and youths 2–17 years in NHANES II and HHANES. *Human Biology, 60:* 205–222, 1988.

Mulvihill, J. J., and Smith, D. W.: The genesis of dermatoglyphics. *Journal of Pediatrics, 75:* 579–589, 1969.

Niswander, J. D., Barrow, M. V., and Bingle, G. J.: Congenital malformations in the American Indian. *Social Biology, 22:* 203–215, 1975.

Polednak, A. P.: Birth defects in Blacks and Whites in relation to prenatal development: a review and hypothesis. *Human Biology, 58:* 317–335, 1986.

Polednak, A. P.: Connective tissue responses in Blacks in relation to disease: further observations. *American Journal of Physical Anthropology, 74:* 357–371, 1987.

Pollitzer, W.: The Negroes of Charleston (S. C.): a study of hemoglobin types, serology, and morphology. *American Journal of Physical Anthropology, 16:* 241–263, 1958.

Roberts, D. F.: Race, genetics and growth. *Journal of Biological Science Supplement, 1:* 43–67, 1969.

Roche, M. B., and Rowe, G. G.: The incidence of separate neural arch and coincident bone variations. A survey of 4,200 skeletons. *Anatomical Record, 109:* 233–252, 1951.

Spurgeon, J. H., Meredith, H. V., and Onouha, G. B. I.: Skin color comparisons among ethnic groups of college men. *American Journal of Physical Anthropology, 64:* 413–418, 1984.

Tanner, J. M., Hayashi, T., Preece, M. A., and Cameron, N.: Increase in length of leg relative to trunk in Japanese children and adults from 1957 to 1977: comparison with British and Japanese Americans. *Annals of Human Biology, 9:* 411–424, 1982.

Thorland, W. G., Johnson, G. O., Housh, T. J., and Refsell, M. J.: Anthropometric characteristics of elite adolescent competitive swimmers. *Human Biology, 55:* 735–748, 1983.

Underwood, Jane H.: *Human Variation and Human Micro-Evolution.* Englewood Cliffs, Prentice-Hall, 1979.

Vickery, S. R., Cureton, K. J., and Collins, M. A.: Prediction of body density from skinfolds in Black and White young men. *Human Biology, 60:* 135–149, 1988.

Wienker, C. W.: Admixture in a biologically African caste of Black Americans. *American Journal of Physical Anthropology, 74:* 265–273, 1987.

Workman, P. L., Blumberg, B. S., and Cooper, A. J.: Selection, gene migration and polymorphic stability in a US White and Negro population. *American Journal of Human Genetics, 15:* 429–437, 1963.

INDEX